For Jacs

BED OF NAILS

PETER OWEN JONES

A LION BOOK

Copyright © 1996 Peter Owen Jones
This edition copyright © 1996 Lion Publishing

The author asserts the moral right
to be identified as the author of this work

Published by
Lion Publishing plc
Sandy Lane West, Oxford, England
ISBN 0 7459 3627 X
Albatross Books Pty Ltd
PO Box 320, Sutherland, NSW 2232, Australia
ISBN 0 7324 1481 4

First edition 1996
10 9 8 7 6 5 4 3 2 1 0

All rights reserved

A catalogue record for this book is available
from the British Library

Printed and bound in Great Britain
by Biddles Ltd, Guildford and Kings Lynn

Introduction

My father was a doctor; he died when I was four. I remember him sitting in the doorway of my bedroom leaning up against the frame, his head lowered. I pushed a toy car across the lino towards him. He picked it up and turned it round, and as he pushed it back he fell forward into the sunlight that lay in squares on the floor. I had no way of knowing how ill he was; he died the following week.

I never sensed his presence after he died: he really did disappear. I now stand up at funerals and try to convince people that the life of the person they have lost lives with them, will always be part of them. It's something that no one can take away from them; their words, their rage, their laughter and comical inconsistencies join the countless reflections in the mirror of our being. It's unfair in many ways; most people are in real pain: on top of this they are slow-marched into an alien environment, drugged on symbolism and told that God loves them and heaven is within touching distance.

What they don't see is the priest having breakfast in the morning, driving alone to the funeral. They don't hear the prayers that are inspired by their tears. They cannot know the conflicts that crackle inside us and the nature of the journeys we have made to reach them. It all looks organized, confident even. They are not allowed to sense any doubt or any of the questions that pour out of our hearts; these are largely out of bounds.

Much like an advertisement, the public are presented with the prepared: the approved and pristine version of the church, the 'here's the one I made earlier'. You end up with the finished article not knowing how it came into being or that much of it is covered in blood.

This manufactured line, which I'm afraid has become a dividing line between you and me, is almost invisible; it weaves its way through human history leaving its visions of God littered in the brittle pages of prayer books and the peeling paint of churches that are now no more than sculptured memorials to the spoils of power and the fading scent of certainty.

Clearly the church has always been passionate about itself, less so more recently perhaps. But it is still this passion that dictates the God you see, the God you perhaps love or hate and at worst are utterly indifferent about.

Maybe you've never thought of a priest as being passionate. The insipid or perverted model served up by the media is completely unrepresentative: no surprises on that front. The media priest serves the media, no one else. They publicly hang us from time to time. I'm not going to get sentimental about it other than to say that with the church reduced to the ridiculous, thorny questions of morality and ethics can be conveniently ignored.

Priests, vicars, ministers, whatever you want to call them, are buffeted through the same cultural scrum as everyone else; we see the same commercials. We buy wrapping paper at Christmas and cry when it hurts. God comes peering through the looking glass of this culture either smiling or screaming, in pain or in love. However, our society, I believe, determines who the priests are, what we are and where the boundaries lie. At best it's an exchange of ideas based on practical necessity. However, I have become increasingly convinced that the Church of England has sold its soul to the emporium emperors, that the ransom we pay for our existence has become our *raison d'être*, that the balance between church and society has been surrendered. We have God, you have everything else. Yes, there are pious souls who soap-box on about God having us, leading us, loving us, and in the darkness that from time to time envelopes our lives there is perhaps no other response. But for the most part we sell you God, you buy him when you have to, when you need him/her. What you see of God is dictated by the church and those who make him their business. The God you buy has gone through agony to get to you, not only on the cross of Jesus Christ but also suffering the intricacies of our own arrogance which spills over into indifferent barbarism and paralysing emptiness.

The God you see has been carefully constructed: his eyes, his lips, his touch, his voice and his words. That doesn't make him unreal; it is our description of him that makes him uncertain. He is flawed by our human eyes, our lips, our touch, our voice and our words. The church is constantly grappling with the myriad of words and images that come flooding through history and the faces and thoughts of Christ that haunt the hearts of each generation.

At theological college these conflicting images and cultures collide. The past, the present, the punk, the puritan, the spiritual. They are all there, rubbing shoulders with each other, jockeying for the right to be believed. This book is about that conflict.

All theological colleges are different. They each have their own agenda, their preferred pictures of God and their own pin-up priests. This book also reflects my own prejudices and the prejudices of the college I was at.

Christianity cannot escape from the characters that present it. It is tied to their beauty and their failings, it is their quirks and their certainties that have given birth to their church. History is pregnant with the lives of the rotten, the ridiculous and pious Christians. Clearly some of us are called to be both rotten and ridiculous. As a child of my generation I bring to God cultural influences unique not only to me but also to this generation.

The resonance of God at some point in the future will be determined for a brief moment at least by our vision of him, of her.

The God that led me to the gates of theological college was the father I did not know, not in the sense that he was in any way distant; more perhaps that I hadn't had the courage before to look into those eyes.

Theological college forces you to confront the boundaries you place around God: most of us keep him locked in a cage, which we refer to pervertedly as our soul. It also removes the boundaries placed around him by other people and reveals just how far they are prepared to go before it gets uncomfortable. These boundaries are really our own weaknesses and in that sense they are perhaps medicinal; they undress us from our robes, ridicule our theories and drag us into the gutter where most of us really belong; they break us if we are bold enough to let them.

I also think it is critical to view Christianity not only as a faith but also as a separate culture with its own language, teapots, mannerisms and dress sense. With the church increasingly adopting the mantle of a minority mentality our cultural quirks are in danger of becoming cast in stone.

Theological college for me was an introduction to Christian culture: the peer groups, the perfume, the periodicals and the puke-coloured book covers embroidered with sunsets and saccharin smiles.

Hand in glove with some of the most interesting colour combinations I've ever seen was the academic work. I left school, shall we say, at sixteen. I had no idea how important academic study is and this book owes much of its substance to the most inspirational teaching and gentle patience I have ever experienced.

Ripe within its pages, I'm afraid, are also my own boundaries. It is only impartial in the sense that it is naive and what is written is a true account of my experience. I wrote it to make money and in some way to try and heal the divide and dismantle the fences between those of us who have God and those of us who don't. It was initially simply meant to be a diary that explained the nuts and bolts of theological training and the first third of the book really reflects how little I knew of the variety of traditions and numbing niceties that infect the Christian faith. It really took about six months for the novelty of being immersed in Nitromorse to wear off and the regulation smiles to wear thin. I began to realize after that that this wasn't meant to be fun and that my own relationship with God was also being threatened, challenged and enriched. My boundaries, the boundaries I place around my faith were also under attack. I can't say I really wrote this book; it was a book that wrote itself. I must also add that some of the opinions that are expressed within the book I am unable to support any more; they are, however, what I felt at the time.

I would like to thank Peter Raynor, my first English teacher, Michael Thomas and Maurice Lyon for their support, Freda Hemmaway for all the hours she spent patiently deciphering my dreadful handwriting and Ann Gordon for picking up her charcoals.

Day One

'4 o'clock tea on the lawn followed by College Communion'. This was my invitation to theological college. Anything the Church of England does which involves tea usually means a gathering of a strange sub-group of human beings who generally have the dress sense of garden gnomes. Church of England crockery also has its own distinctive shine; it's either that regulation 'church hall ware' which is usually an off-white glass hybrid that sets your teeth on edge just by looking at it or a motley collection of mugs hewn from trade fairs, day trips and the back-end of birthdays. We had the white stuff. Dressing for the occasion had its own unique problems. Do you go 'à la shock': 'Hey cookie, get a load of these leopard skin trousers!' or do you go for the Mr Sensible outfit? We decided on the safe option but we still, I think, looked like gatecrashers on what resembled the annual dinner and dance of the Synthetic Fibres Association.

We had arrived. Judging by the look on my wife's face we'd arrived in hell. My worst fears were confirmed when having been directed to the common room we were greeted by a man who had a goatee beard, green trousers and a purple jacket. I'm afraid I bypassed his outstretched hand and fled in the direction of the teacups. Mingling on the lawn was also difficult. There were the usual English rituals of trying to greet one another with a partially frozen sausage roll in one hand and a cup of tea in the other.

The most worrying thing however is that, for some as yet unknown reason, potential vicars all look like potential vicars. It is the easiest thing in the world to throw your mind forward and observe the gathered throng in surplice, holding their arms up to the Lord. After what seemed an eternity of pleasantries we were officially welcomed by a man with a round face and enthusiastic eyes who then introduced us all to the Principal. It was at this point that all my social nightmares were realized as the man with the goatee beard, green trousers and purple jacket assured us he knew about as much as we did and he too was finding his way around. We were all then ushered into Chapel, which was nothing other than sheer relief at not having to smile at people, there were no names to remember, no gaping errors to make. The singing was wonderful, the light on the stone floor was even better.

Day Two

There is a Chapel service every morning at eight-fifteen. This is something that will happen every morning in term time for the next two years. To be frank, this is a fine thing: for starters it gets it out of the way and secondly once your system recovers from the initial shock, it will hopefully serve to remind me as to the real reason why I'm here. The fact that it is well attended might have something to do with the fact that it's compulsory, but that doesn't seem to deter the odd bunk here and there.

After Chapel there was a series of complicated introductions. The tutors sat in chairs facing us in a room with a high ceiling and huge windows crammed with lead: it smelt serious. We were then set upon by all of them in turn—the routine was pretty much the same—they waved paper at us and recommended a million books.

By far the most complicated system to master was the meals. We were all allowed twenty-five credits per week. Sounds simple enough. However, when you actually have to juggle the culinary complexities of one meal being worth two and a half credits, except on Friday when meals are three and a half credits, children are half a credit, not to mention the fact that LF is low fat, V is vegetarian, LFV is low fat vegetarian, it smacks of theory that collapses in practice. We'll see.

In the afternoon we were given a tour of the library. It was utterly meaningless. I didn't even understand the categories, and the writers that shot out lovingly from between the lips of the large Australian lecturer could have been ice cream flavours for all I knew.

Day Three

I spent most of today calling Gordon, Andrew; David, Michael and Sean, Kevin. Most people end up asking each other the same question at least six times and only then does everything seem to sort itself out.

We are all allocated a Chapel group which at some stage during the term has to dream up the shape and content of a job lot of and, in our case, the inner plumbing of, an imminent Communion Service, so in the late morning we sat entombed in the book-encrusted lair of the generously-proportioned barnacle-featured church history tutor's room. The debate was whether the service should centre round creation or mission. After some initial forays into theological point scoring, the creationists won having cited Calvin's interpretation of the word 'dominion' as being something far more contemporary than the Calvinisation of an obscure African missionary. I had absolutely no idea what any of them were talking about. The conversation might as well have been conducted in Romanian.

The main event this afternoon was an interview with the three main tutors. I duly waited my turn. We had to sort out a parish placement, a pastoral study and a mission and go through a strange system of points that needed to be reached before I could be summarily sent out on my first curacy. It was here that I first encountered the reclined theological position.

It seemed the lower down you sat in a chair, the closer to God you in fact were. For someone not imbued with as many vertical inches as I might have wished for, this was a surreal experience. I spent half an hour talking to people's heads just visible above the arms of the armchairs they were occupying. I was assured that this wasn't meant to be intimidating.

After we had travelled around the endless computations of pastoral studies clashing with missions, and bereavement counselling falling on the same night as 'Match of the Day', we mutually arrived at the master plan. Pastoral studies placement in the Easter, mission in the summer, sociology, New Testament studies, Old Testament studies and pastoral studies in some sort of digestible order. Into that had also to be fitted Bible study, football, music, a parish placement and—what should have been first on the list—my family. I was assured it would be good training for ministry.

Groupings among the students are now beginning to emerge: Fundamentalists, Fundamental Evangelicals, Evangelicals, Liberal Evangelicals, Liberals, High-Churchers, Low-Churchers, not to mention raving Charismatics, are all beginning to whisper in pockets. There is common ground, which is an amazing thing in itself because the mix of professions and backgrounds is as diverse as it is unlikely. When you add a dash of political persuasion to this melting pot the results are nothing short of astonishing, crossing all cultural, ethnic and regional boundaries. There are chartered surveyors, barristers, a footballer, several social workers, a tree surgeon, a medic, a sprinkling of teachers, a psychiatric nurse, an engineer and many others who under the normal scheme of things would never have met, let alone made each other cups of tea and confessed to supporting Crystal Palace. I'm sharing a study with this bloke who looks like a mature and sensible version of Bart Simpson. He's an ex-physics graduate from Cambridge. We have absolutely nothing in common except for the fact that his wife used to live near East Grinstead; he's brimming with books, they're everywhere. I've agreed not to smoke in the study. I think he's very shy.

There is a great sense of welcome. There needs to be; our lives will never be the same. We've stepped over an invisible canyon. The way back is littered with the violence of the shadows we've left behind. I am lonely—they told us we would be. I have found this alley where I go and smoke and give my smiling face a rest. It's the only place of real quiet. It's somewhere to touch God again.

Day Four

This morning we were all squeezed into the unfortunately named 'Rank Room', nerve centre of the Methodists' theological college. The Methodists really do have an edge in terms of attire. I don't think there was one natural fibre between them; even their shoes appeared to be a combination of recycled pub carpets and shower curtains. The session started with a briefing on the life, low-life and realities of the city we had all recently acquired membership of. First off was the Mayor, a nice enough bloke, living proof really that by keeping your nose clean and speaking slowly anyone can do it. Second on was our local MP, our new local MP in fact. Again no stunning insights on that front. They both appeared to be in competition to persuade us how bad, depraved and violent this politically famous corner of England was and all we had to do was scratch the surface to release all sorts of ugly tensions, muggings and a proliferation of poverty-stricken one-parent families.

On that high note the floor was invited to question our visiting speakers. The best we managed was the politically challenging inquisition as to why the bicycle lane had been closed in the centre of town.

We had lunch in the Methodists' dining hall. I was advised in the queue by a whispering Anglican that Methodist meals had far too much in common with their shoes. As an institution its corridors are quiet, the walls are cold, there was dust on the stairs. Everything felt rationed. The tea was weak. The highlight of the afternoon was the almost vitriolic ramblings of an ordained economics lecturer turned monk who informed us that theology was by and large a complete nonsense and that Christianity was about living it. Half the audience loved it. The other half fidgeted uncomfortably without smiling once.

This evening those of us who had just joined were crammed into the Principal's flat and fed sweet and sour pork, a crate full of prawn crackers and several buckets of rice and beef noodles. The evening was billed as a warts and all introduction to theological college where those who had suffered the previous year stood up and told us all how. I can't say there were that many warts, which worried me. Reading between the lines I can't help thinking that I'm merely waiting for a bomb to go off inside me; no one has said anything remotely honest yet, especially about their feelings, and that worries me. There are moments when I feel like I've been transported to cloud-cuckoo-land.

The first week has finished: my main recollections are of corridors, high ceilings, stern stained-glass windows and tense faces. It's hard to run an establishment of sixty or so people without it somewhere along the line leaving a smell of school mince in the air. However personal, however Christian, this is an institution with its own unique language, quirks, humour and ethics.

Our Principal assured us he was keen to take the best from the past and make it relevant for the future. All the thys, thees and thous, all of it: comforting, yes; pretty, yes; relevant, I don't know, probably not. I have two years to chew it over.

Week Two

After morning prayers, we had a free day of sorts. Lectures begin tomorrow: Old Testament studies, five past nine. So, today's efforts were really spent on football and music practice.

One of the great things about study is what happens when you're not studying: to have a football fixture list, music practice, flower arranging and as many societies crying out for you to join them as there are fleas on a hedgehog, is an immense luxury and one I am determined to indulge in.

Football practice was interesting. The standard was very high and, here comes the big one, no fouls, no 'Oh come on ref he was miles offside'; no one whispering 'Short-arse' in your ear, no acrobatics in the penalty area. Doesn't sound like football, does it? Our first match is on Monday against a team from the Council, most of whom are dustmen. Back to reality. Boy, do we need it.

Tuesday, Week Two

The book-list handed to us in the first lecture this morning was just under, in terms of volume, two full sides of A4. I have not read that many books in my entire life.

After lunch we had what is called a common room meeting. No staff are allowed. This is entirely a student affair where such matters as the bar, the scandal of surplus meal credits, and tat are discussed (Tat is the term used for cassocks and surplices.) These items of clothing retail at around £300; gobsmacked! I was swallowing flies. When you consider that the grant gives a family with one child just over £120 a week to live on (that's everything: rent, bills, food, clothes, birthday presents, stationery, not forgetting books) per week, £300 is a huge sum which I don't know at present how I'm going to find. That bridge will have to be crossed in the future.

To encourage a spirit of mutual dependence, there are deacons appointed for just about every conceivable task. There's a bicycle deacon, a mission deacon and an archdeacon who's the senior student elected by the students, for the students. There's a food deacon, a worship deacon, and a whole host of other deacons all helping all the other deacons to live, eat, ride bicycles, drink beer and praise the Lord.

This afternoon I had my first appointment with what's called a pastoral tutor. Pastoral tutors differ from the teaching kind. Their brief is your emotional and spiritual well-being. I cannot underplay the magnitude of the culture shock that lies in wait at theological college, especially if you've been earning a crust out there for several years. I'm sure everyone thinks 'no problems', it's just a different set of faces. It's much more. For a start, you do genuinely become part of a Christian community. This is a huge step to take. It's like moving from a madhouse into a monastery. Now, that's not a reflection on those beyond the walls, it's more of a reflection on the monastery. To a large extent there's no escape, no mental escape. God has your undivided attention for a very large part of your day, and it is probably coming to terms with the reality of this that I would imagine for some people is a leap into the vast beyond; for me this is definitely the case. I like my pastoral tutor. I'm not sure I would tell him everything, but I could tell him most things if I had to. We live in a society where nobody really tells anybody anything anymore. Few of us have the courage to divulge the madness that mauls our insides; the adultery we commit on the bus is done in the shadows of our being, our dreams are sealed behind our eyes. Christ perhaps is so potent because he sees all of this in us; we keep it from most people. My study-mate Bart and I almost had a conversation this afternoon. His road to faith is so different from mine that they might as well have been engineered on different planets. He is a deeply moral man and it has been that morality that has taken him to Christ. I on the other hand have been dragged kicking and screaming out of some of the less salubrious haunts of this country and am really here by default.

After Bart was New Testament studies and after that we all adjourned to the coffee bar in town and exchanged our 'how we ended up here' stories. The church put you through this process of interviews where everything, from your sexual orientation to how much earwax you produce, is discussed in minute detail. We all agreed the only way to stay sane was not to give yourself up, earwax and all, to the college. Outside friends were not only important sources of life, but reminded you that most people do drink, smoke, swear and buy clothes that haven't just walked off a Seventies' golf course. The general Synod vote on the ordination of women is imminent. Regardless of my own particular feelings, it is the women of the college who, by and large, are living without fingernails. Being sentenced to a never-ending curacy takes in my view immense courage; even more so when you are convinced that your calling is for the whole shooting match, the full monty. It's a hard pill to swallow. Who knows whether these women will have to take it after November the twelfth?

October 1992

The lecturer this morning was very bloody good. No frills, no disappearing off onto some academic cloud; just straight from the hip, wallop. Look at text, look at content, bang. The epistles are letters, we don't know the replies, pow.

The main problem of the day has come from Joanna Trollope. *The Rector's Wife* is sending Richter Scale 8.9 shockwaves through this ecclesiastical community. Mainly because it at last shows up, with a fair share of literary licence, the miserable lot of women married to miserable vicars. The poverty, the petty careerism and all that baggage that most vicars hide under their cassocks. Partners, as they are inclusively called at the moment, do not have an easy time of things. This is down to the church's inability to challenge the popular misconception that, simply because someone is married to a vicar, it makes them part of the parish. There has been some fence-sitting on this front of quite spectacular proportions. I think the public want to keep the vicar's wife as a sort of relic of forever England, something the tabloids can bait, something that acts as a reassuring sign that nothing has changed.

My wife is not typical. However, many partners are, and are also very eager to throw themselves at counselling courses, autopsies and the social fabric of the college, which is fine and admirable. What is not so admirable is that you can't help feeling that somewhere along the line, the performance of your partner is being judged alongside that of your own. I'm afraid I cannot accept even a hint of this. My wife is her own person, an individual more than capable of deciding what she wants and how she wants it. I love her madly and if by choice she chooses to become involved, that's fine. However, if by choice she chooses not to be involved, that is also fine, very fine by me.

There is a partners' group here, a very active one. They invite guest speakers to illuminate on everything from child abuse to one hundred ways with rice. Before we arrived here my wife had a letter from another woman in the group introducing herself and making lots of encouraging noises. Within these walls my wife would not be termed a Christian so the glue that holds everything together here doesn't work on her. She is in the unenviable position of having been transported to a strange town where the only chance of any real social interaction is with a bunch of people who would prefer to swim in Jacob's Creek rather than drink it and, for the most part, are in her eyes clinically insane. This evening the guests were none other than the Principal and his wife shooting from the hip about life on the wrong side of the tracks in Gillingham. She listened.

On Tuesday evenings all shades and colours of Christianity are forced to endure the snappily titled 'Federation Eucharist'. I had had enough so I bunked it. To be honest, you get pretty churched-out here and, worst of all, you become discerning, looking for the next heavy hit of Christianity.

A church service serving different traditions within the Anglican movement that is designed not to offend any of the competing flavours achieves the notable distinction of being utterly tasteless. Throw incense at me, shout from the pulpit, but not this, not this numbing necessity.

I bought a file today with some dividers. It's come to that: essay titles, Bible study notes. It's all happening, happening with a bang. We looked at Revelation chapter 12 in an exercise designed to demonstrate that it is possible to extract sense from the oblique without relying on commentaries and the professional genius of lecturers. That was the theory. Naturally, it's impossible. We all dived in with our emerging theology held aloft, only to find that we were, all of us, quite wrong and it meant exactly the opposite to what we thought it did; it was a lively debate though, beautifully chaired.

For lunch there was half a baked potato and some salad. The food here is very good. There's never any left. Lunch is always interrupted by announcements. Today's was that a prowler was lurking in the grounds of the college; medium height, longish brownish hair and a beard, and was wearing scruffy clothes. Last year the same prowler had been spotted and the same announcement made.

After lunch, a particularly vigilant ordinand had spotted the offender down by the washing machines, going into the lavatories. He waited outside and challenged the man, asking him to leave immediately. Apparently, it took at least five minutes for the man in question to explain he wasn't here to steal the cutlery, he was in fact here for an interview to be the new principal of the college. He was the one that got the job.

We were back on Revelation this afternoon. It is, beyond the theology, an immense piece of writing, unique, bold, secretive and dripping with imagination. My head was actually reeling by the end of it, our first match against the Council however returned it to its usual state. I was substituted at half time, nobody's fault, having squandered three open goals and having been nutmegged more times than a croquet hoop. The captain had little alternative other than to present me with the linesman's flag.

Our group prayers this morning were not without incident. We all take it in turns to host these Friday morning sessions and this morning it was the turn of one of our number called 'Mad Dog'. The whole problem stemmed from 'God the Mother', as opposed to God the Father. The Hebrew word in the Bible, and apparently some of the Greek words, used to describe the 'Holy Spirit' are, according to Mad Dog, feminine. This theological assumption clearly did nothing for Bart and a couple of the others who said, quite plainly, they believed God was a man and that was that. In short, any reference to God in the feminine emerged out of New Age sympathy and was trendy and should be disregarded as such. Mad Dog stood his ground. I did see him twitch a couple of times. He looks like a man who has had too many electric shocks. The compromise which was deftly engineered by my pastoral tutor was that those who did not agree did not have to say the offending lines on the offending prayer sheet. The result was that it then became incredibly obvious who did agree and who didn't.

After the delights of Zwingli and the punk Anabaptist reformers I headed off unannounced down to London. It was on the train that I realized I hadn't actually been anywhere for far too long. Theological college can consume you—perhaps it is meant to. I'm beginning to feel as if I am in 'no man's land'. What disturbed me the most was how quickly secular life appears secular. Posters advertising bras, cars, chocolates and holidays in the Seychelles seem somehow totally and completely irrelevant. They are not the currency of my life anymore and I will not spill any more blood on their account. The girl in the Miss Selfridge ad is more subtle—her glorious eyes are aimed at your flies (that's when it hits you). You begin to get an inkling that, like it or not, you are being ghettoized. It's a Christian ghetto; a club, a cult but, in the absence of a common faith, a ghetto nevertheless. I so desperately wanted to be the same, but I wasn't. I couldn't be. I had lost the right to ogle at women, get outrageously pissed and wallow in the arms of self-pity. This was serious. The next day I sat alone at lunch ruing my loss. The early Christians didn't pull their punches, they went straight for the jugular. A letter from Peter delivers a telling right hook. It states that to hear the words of Christ and then return to one's old ways is akin to a dog eating its own vomit. I swallowed hard. He's right of course.

November 1992

A journalist from a national newspaper is with us today. I knew him in London, pad in hand, ears on overdrive, every answer to every carefully crafted statement posing yet another mind-boggling difficult moral dilemma. What did I think of drugs, sex before marriage, the miners' strike, Northern Ireland? All relevant, vital and does the church have any answers? The church has never been great on the immediate questions of our time, preferring to either dither or retire to some academic garret and ponder the balance. Anyway, it struck me that we are still involved in a battle between good and evil; the church doesn't make a great deal of that. Doubtless for some watertight reasons.

Journalists tend to smile like angels and bite like dogs. This one was on the trail of the women ordinands, asking why, where and how? He was planning a feature to break just before the vote on the ordination of women. This morning he came to morning prayers which I think fazed him slightly; we all held hands and prayed for each other. His comment was that it was 'earnest'. It was. He then sat in on a lecture of Old Testament history which was a mistake. None of us understood a word of it.

This evening was billed as the 'moveable feast', the idea being that those who live out either cook a main course or a pudding for those who live in, and everyone spends one of the courses at someone else's house. We ordinands are, by and large, not brilliant at letting our hair down. Most of us don't have much to surrender to wild abandon in the first place, but it does get tiring. It's like never being told the punch line of a dirty joke; everybody knows it, we all know that nobody's perfect either, so this jousting for sainthood is meaningless. All we have in common is God and an ardent, passionate desire to do what we are doing. It can overtake everything else. It should; it is a very serious business. The downside of that is that we take ourselves far too seriously. The pressure to conform is intense. Now by and large, it's easy, a joy, the honeymoon continues; but I'm quite sure God wants each of us to be who we are: we can't all be sweet, we can't all like Van Morrison.

The main course was at Mad Dog's house, a small group of us were just about to tuck into the home-made lasagne when he began to tell us about his 'when I was working as a pharmacist' experiences. These, as far as I could make out, largely revolved around women showing him their breasts for what appeared to be no apparent good reason. I then jumped into the car and drove back to my own house where another group of us had fruit salad and ice cream. I'd come to the end really. I'd run out of sugar and witty stories. I just wanted to shake all of them. There was an old priest there, I caught him staring at me a couple of times. At least he was real, his eyes watered reality. I could hear him thinking that we were all dancing to the disco in cloud-cuckoo-land.

To my shock and naked horror, I realized this morning that there are six weeks to go, only six, then Christmas. I've been planning to do things, planning to make a start. In truth, I have done nothing so now I must, there are essay titles flooding round the corridors of this college. Unless I get going, the soup of confusion between Calvin, Zwingli, the Exilic Prophets, counselling, humanity, God, Pink Floyd, and the Sermon on the Mount will doubtless render me frozen forever.

Within this cotton-wool community there is someone whose single purpose is to act as a prayer counsellor. My prayer life has taken off like a rocket since I've been here, mainly because of the amount of quality time that I've been able to give to it. The prayer counsellor is one of those women that you could tell anything to. Anything.

The difference between her room and the rest of the management was that she had a mock coal fire. It was a bit like walking onto the set of 'Sit Up and Listen'. Much like the television programme you knew that this was the end of the line before the transmission went dead; in prayer terms this was the last comfort zone before hell. There were dried flowers neatly arranged in earthy-coloured earthenware vases, just the odd book or two, some off-brownish-pinkish chairs and an almost new carpet.

I could imagine her in Heaven. It was the way she moved. She had a slow smile and powerful eyes. I haven't thought that much about Heaven, but if I made it there, which is highly unlikely, I know she'd be there too.

Socially, things are still a bit hit and miss. It's not something you can instantly put your finger on although I still feel we are all very much feeling our way. What is amazing is seeing people beginning to open up, beginning to say what they feel, beginning to trust.

Sociology was intriguing: today was myth, symbols and rituals. My, what an impressionable bunch we are. I thought a football match was a glorified sing song with a snippet of football. No, no, quite wrong. I thought 'EastEnders' was a modern soap opera. Wrong again. We are all of us attached to symbols. We were told in hushed tones that nobody talks when the telly's on. Had the sociologists, I wondered seriously, considered the possibility that this might be because nobody could otherwise hear it? Oh no, not in the world of symbol, myth and ritual. This is a ritualistic act whereby we allow ourselves to have our incredulity massaged and our day organized around a specific time, to become part of a world that reinforces our identities of ourselves. Got it. The worrying thing is that this all makes perfect sense. After half an hour of sociology, and quite a bit of languishing in incredulity, most things seem to make sense. I can't help thinking I've been inhabiting some strange world of my own invention, but that's it, I'm tied to my own ritualistic behaviour: it operates unquestioned. The upshot of all of this was, when we do arrive in a parish, we have to discover the myth: what the people of the parish believe it to be. You see, we were told an interesting story of how this missionary in the bygone days of missionaries (the type that didn't travel on aeroplanes) used to lovingly pat all the little boys in an African village on the head. His mission failed. It took the Church of England fifty years to work out that within the tribe, to pat someone on the head is the worst possible insult of all time because in doing so you place a curse on them that they won't grow any taller.

I'd love to score a goal. I'd love to pass the ball effortlessly. I'd love to tackle someone. My footballing skills have run off. At the grand old age of thirty-four, the tank may well be empty. It's a depressing thought. I played appallingly badly.

The photographer from the paper turned up after lunch armed with an arsenal of cameras. He arranged us in the light of the dining room. But I think he settled for the art-house shot, the mean and moody 'don't mess' look draped over the branches of an ancient Virginia creeper. All will doubtless be revealed.

Thursday was busy: Chapel, eight-fifteen; writing intercessions; church history ten o'clock; Old Testament studies, eleven. Then I delivered my first seminar on the plot of Matthew. I'm not convinced my observations comparing the literary quality of Matthew to the lyrics of David Bowie went down that well. Then, after a brief baked potato, salad and quiche, I ran around a football field, chasing the ball and trying to find excuses as to why I never caught up with it. We then had an open debate of sorts on the ordination of women. The highlight of this was when Mad Dog stood up and treated us all to the benefits of a man tying fishing line round his testicles whilst his wife was going through labour. In mid-contraction the wife affectionately pulls hard on the fishing line, causing her husband excruciating pain, the idea being that the pain of childbirth becomes a shared experience. We all then trooped rather gingerly into an environmentally based Eucharist, where I read the intercessions; the service ended. I went home and really that was the last thing I remember.

Friday was educational. Some weeks ago, I volunteered to be the college's AOCM representative. AOCM is a body that represents ordinands' interests to the corridors of power lurking in the church. The venue of the get-together was the one and only Welsh theological college which was tucked away in the back streets of Cardiff. It all really got off to a bad start. I was late and then someone made the fatal mistake of offering me a glass of sherry. If you can imagine the archetypal man, out of all the men on the planet, who is most likely to offer you a glass of sherry, forty-something with drip-dry hair and a mouth full of well-meaning teeth, well, it was him. It didn't help the situation that he was wearing black from head to foot and had the demeanour of the ultimate Seventies 'clock the sideburns' movie baddie. At that exact moment, the whole room stopped talking.

I declined the sherry out of principle. First of all, I think it's bad for sherry and, secondly, it's even worse for the church. It's bad because it's expected, it's unoriginal, it fulfils people's expectations of both. I settled politely for an orange juice.

Another worrying fact is that, once again, it's incredibly obvious that you are standing in a room with fifteen potential vicars, fourteen of them all drinking sherry. It's footwear, isn't it? It's the footwear that does it. It's not that they are wearing it, it's that they actually went out and chose it. Where can one buy shoes that look like they've had a bad trip in a washing machine? And who is it that's selling a nice line in Seventies golf jumpers? I don't know. I didn't ask. As ever, appearances are deceptive, and there were not only some extremely bright thinkers, but also some very capable and forceful speakers. After the pleasantries and some supper we were dispatched. We then had a talk from one of the bigwigs on the Selection Board. I have to say, this was the first time in my entire leanings towards the church that someone has made complete sense for over an hour. It was nothing short of inspirational. It was a privilege to listen to. The culmination really was this: it is in essence a sacrifice to become a vicar, to take any holy orders you have to give up a part of you, it is not an easy thing to do. Maybe that is why, to start with, it is such an isolating experience.

Now, being stupid, I hadn't even thought about it. It is, of course, an incredible privilege but it doesn't mean it's easy. I don't think any of the ordinands I have met so far in any way find what they are doing an easy thing to do. You are racked with doubt and as your faith grows, so do your doubts: they both become powerful, both beautiful and telling. We still have an immense communication problem to overcome.

The reality of the Holy Spirit is so immense, so astounding; we are barely equipped to talk about it. Yes, there are books on prayer but we are very bad at being able to talk about feelings, the reality of our relationship with God through Christ. Now, it's easy to write that and it all sounds very neat but we seem unable to discuss the overpowering sensation of love, the conscious experience of total confidence in guidance and nurture. In short, we are failing to demonstrate that this is a real, living, doing, loving, selfish, bloody awful, intensely beautiful, overpowering battle of wills. Christians stand up and say God is here, now. Christ is with us. Yes, he is. Yes, they are, but unless you have experienced the reality of those statements, it becomes rather like watching an advertisement for soap powder when you have no understanding of the concept of clothes. The decisions ordinands make draw them irrevocably closer, with all the dangers that entails, to the Holy Spirit. There are some people who say the church is dead, it's the Tory Party at prayer, it's outmoded, outdated, it's been outlawed. Yes, it's all of those things but the people of the church are in fact, by even the most modest standards, doing an immensely radical thing. Maybe that is why outwardly at least they are not radical people. I have some Bible notes to write.

Yesterday was manic, today was studious. Monday is always busy. Well, I've written it, the first essay. I haven't edited it yet. I'll do that tomorrow. I'm pleased I've broken the back of it.

Sociology was very dull this morning. Are sociologists fundamentally bored? I mean, we could all invent theories for this and that and for why my lampstand is in a particular place, but it's too difficult to remember. You have to remember to approach the problem sociologically before you can reap the benefits of your sociological observations, otherwise it becomes like forgetting where you put your shoes every morning. Okay, it's not all grim but I did spend half the lecture watching this man fighting sleep. He was brave. He did everything humanly possible to stave off the eyes closing and the jaw dropping. He changed positions. He took his glasses off. He asked several pointless questions. He put his glasses back on again. Eventually, about four minutes before the end of the lecture, he was overcome and fell asleep sitting bolt upright, holding his pen, with his head drooping over his paper. The lecturer didn't notice a thing.

The real highlight yesterday was a chat with the Poacher and a couple of others in the pub. The Poacher is a large Devonian whose father and brother are also men of the cloth. We tend to sit at the back in lectures passing puerile pieces of paper between us. He used to be a tree surgeon; we have conversations at lunch about the romance of rural ministry and wild mushrooms. He told me yesterday that a pint of Wadworth 6X was 'alive with the glory of God'. I'm not sure how many he had had by then. He has a chequered history, a lurcher dog and a laugh that touches his toes. There are definite groupings now. I have to say that the Conservative Evangelicals seem to be the most vociferous. This naturally is not an easy thing to deal with if you are more of a pub person. I do have a bigger worry though, and that is, sense of humour. I don't believe that God intended all Christians to have to giggle inanely at the word 'bollocks'. 'Bollocks' in itself is not a particularly funny word unless you have the comic timing of Griff Rhys Jones, but it's as if there is something slightly naughty about the 'b' word and that one only hears it after two glasses of wine, which probably explains the inane giggling. The moment you become a serious Christian it appears that you either have a sense of humour by-pass or that Sooty and Sweep seem, for some unknown reason, to become very funny indeed.

Today we had a common room meeting. Mad Dog had erected a board between the common room and the dining room and was lobbying for support from all who would listen for his 'mission lunches' which we were all due to vote on. I delivered my report from what was said in Wales which was basically a plea for realism for those looking for curacies and that not all of them could be in a three-bedroom house near the pub, four hundred yards from a Tandoori restaurant in an Evangelical church which had a nationally acclaimed school attached to it.

The Church Inspectors, we learned, had decided we should have one social evening, at least, per term, which everyone was duty-bound to attend. I wasn't so much surprised at the total lack of understanding the stipulation revealed, more the arrogance of it. You shall all meet in a room. You shall talk together and share your experiences. You shall all have a good time. You shall all eat chicken fricassee. To believe that anyone is going to be relaxed and enjoying themselves when they have been forced to do something they quite clearly do not want to do is doolally. We voted it down. Mad Dog's also scored a notable victory in forcing everyone to voluntarily have soup and a roll on Fridays, the money saved going to charity.

Well, it came out today. The picture just about covered a bigger surface area than the copy. On reflection, I think it was very fair; a few people were uptight about a couple of theological misunderstandings. The Eucharist had become Evensong; the cooking didn't go down a bundle either—the potatoes were described as being 'as hard as bullets', which was a fair description of Mad Dog's culinary prowess (he was cooking the common room supper that night). I'm not sure that I didn't commit credibility suicide by putting the earliest recollections of my calling down to 'copious amounts of cannabis'. But it was all said in a very positive piece of journalism, a rare coup for the Church of England.

One's calling still remains a mystery in a sense. Maybe it will always be so. I can remember quite clearly feeling very strongly indeed, it was almost physical at times, that I had to spend my life as a vicar. It would have been far better, I feel, if I had been a practising Christian. Maybe I would have accepted it more readily. I still regard the whole episode with awe almost, as if it didn't happen to me. I know that it did and, although the temptation to post-rationalize experience, especially religious experience, into understandable packages is a common human failing, what I'm doing now is the only thing I have done that feels right for me. One of my best friends once described falling in love as a complicated key fitting into a complicated lock and opening it as only that key could. It is a remarkable description and much of me feels the same way about what's happening now.

We always fight so hard for what we want, for what we think we need. It's that, more than anything, that gets in the way of the Holy Spirit trying desperately to get through to you. Throughout the ages, men and women have been called by God to serve him/her and, in doing so, dedicate their lives to serving others. The fact that it's happened, the fact that it's happening now, the reality that ordinary people like myself feel compelled, through a number of different religious experiences, to follow up that calling is, for me, one of the greatest revelations of the presence of Christ in our midst. We're all different. None of us are perfect. Some of us are far from it, we lose patience with each other, with all the natural things that happen whenever human beings get together. For those people who doubt the existence of God and level at those who don't that they are leading narrow-minded and sheltered lives, I would like to say this: it is those who do believe who are living right out on the edge. Becoming a vicar is a very radical thing to do, it's not a safe and easy option. Once upon a time it might have been, but it's very different now and it's you who are way out of touch.

We lost 4:3. It was a very tight game, very tight. We should have lost 10:3 if it hadn't been for some superb acrobatics by our rookie goalie. Mondays are manic. We had a fine sociology lecture this morning, discussing divorce, marriage, figures, theories, statistics. The lecturer made one incredibly potent remark. He said most churches marry virgins. He was implying that the church really had no way other than outright refusal to marry anyone who was less than spotless. He didn't seem in favour of the blind eye approach. Monday's New Testament studies ended with yet another substantial question which was, again, on the question of marriage: 'Do the Gospels hide a more radical Jesus?' This was again noted because of the discrepancy in commentaries between Matthew and Mark concerning divorce.

I have to admit I'm in a dilemma here if Christ stated that divorce is wrong. Moreover, adultery is done with the heart and mind. Then we have slipped, slipped badly. The realities of society paint a far from perfect picture. What is the church to do? Refuse to marry people? Refuse to marry a divorced woman whose previous drunken husband knocked her about black and blue? Refuse to marry a man whose previous wife runs off with the local bouncer? The Scriptures would say unequivocally, yes. There's no doubt about it. I don't know I'm afraid, but I take the man's point. Turning a blind eye serves nobody, nobody at all.

Synod votes tomorrow on the ordination of women. It is a monumental decision that will change the church for ever. We have a prayer vigil all day. I'm in favour. Nobody has any idea which way the vote will go. Whatever happens, there will be hurt and pain on both sides. Someone has to lose. Should it have come to this?

The Day of the Vote

Two votes. It was two votes, that's all. What a joy. I sat in front of the telly crying like a baby. I then drove like a maniac into college and insisted on hugging any woman I could find, which was not a good idea because it set me off again. Well, it's done now so let's get on with it for better or for worse. I have immense sympathy for those who feel they are unable to continue. All I would say is that there is much I disagree with as well, but that I believe we act as a community and it's as a community that we must move forward; Anglo-Catholics, Evangelicals, Charismatics, all of us. What a momentous day.

Can you believe it? We were there, one up at half time. Ten minutes before the end, after a peach of an own goal, we were four-three down. We managed to pull one back, which took it to four all. It was a point.

The Old Testament lecturer announced today that we were going back to the beginning of the Old Testament. We'd started in the middle. I still can't fathom out why we started in the middle but I learnt this morning that we had done. I actually thought it would be very dull, the Old Testament; it isn't, it's fascinating. Once you really get inside it, it becomes more and more remarkable. It must have taken an act of the Divine to persuade the Jews, whose history it is, that Christ was the Messiah. They must have been immensely brave people.

It was after the New Testament seminar that my thoughts really crystallized. I was concerned initially that by picking the Bible to academic pieces it would mathematize and demystify much of what it says. In fact, the reverse has happened. I can now quite understand why some of those who translate the Bible as an academic act end up being converted by it. It is quite immense, not only as divine scripture but also as a witness to humanity's struggle with it. And the further one delves, the greater the sense that revelation is a process that we are all involved in. It is the process of God's revelation that I believe the Bible demonstrates.

After Old Testament studies this morning we all piled over the road into a coffee bar. One of the female ordinands was saying that with all this love, sensitivity and reconciliation, it was actually difficult to express undiluted joy about the vote at Synod, which was a bit of a worry. I also discovered that I am severely out of step on this issue of the community evening. Most people think it is a good idea. I'm not convinced. If they in any way resemble common-room suppers, I don't see them lasting that long.

There are under four weeks to go. It feels some way off yet. Most people have got 'submerged syndrome'. The sheer weight of information they have taken on board, and the knowledge that there are four more weeks of it is, I think, beginning to take its toll. My mother came to lunch today and in passing asked me what I had done this morning; I honestly couldn't remember. I was in no-man's-land, a place in between Mary Queen of Scots, Polycarp and the redaction of the Synoptic Gospels.

At the hall meeting, the Principal outlined as politely as possible the failing of the Bishop's report on theological colleges. Three had been recommended for closure. However, the report was so bad that even the General Synod had failed to take notice of it. This is akin to a vote of no confidence in the Government of the day. After huge amounts of effort, a thousand forms, a spectacularly meaningless cover design, heartache and fingernail biting, two years down the line, his message was that we are effectively back to square one. This was either the worst or the best possible result. There is no decision on the final decision to take the final decision. What a cock-up. This hall meeting had followed a very illuminating session with my sociology tutor who was a great deal more lucid on the internal plumbing of the Church of England.

Both results, I have to say, were equally alarming for different reasons. My sociology tutor, whose voice dropped a decibel every time she hit me with another reality bombshell, was indeed an education. Now, I know sociology lectures have traditionally been left of Lenin; this one was way past politics. The mental state of the church resembles that of the monks a month prior to the dissolution of the monasteries: vicars banished to the South of France, depressed vicars, overworked vicars, inept bishops, supreme politicking. A complete shambles in fact. I loved it.

I'm in the unique position of being naive, enthusiastic and believing in God. This is a rarefied mixture apparently. The ageing ratio goes something like this: as a curate, I can expect to age just about naturally; as a vicar I'm destined to age ten years in five; and as a bishop, it looks like I'm up for twenty years in two, which explains why they all look like badly assembled robots. As for being naive, enthusiastic and in love with Jesus, this apparently doesn't last.

December 1992

I failed the essay. Miserable. I didn't back up any observations with any relevant textual references. I attacked the grand scheme, dealt in generalities and failed to dissect the plethora of implications. I'm not alone—the Poacher's efforts also fell on stony ground. We sat in my study, his large frame hunched up in a small chair, being briefed as to exactly why this had happened. Bart, who passed with distinction, made a diplomatic exit. Once the tutor had actually explained all the points I'd missed, Genesis 1—11 became a whole different ball game. I was flying to the moon. He was off to Pluto with ambitions for Alpha Centauri. I'm seriously considering redoing it. I'll see how it feels after church history next week.

I've done nothing today. The man in the grey Terylene trousers and last year's trainers hit me square between the eyes this morning. The realization that the Gospels give you a loaded four-eyed view of Jesus finally sunk in. We looked at the 'walking on the water' texts. Three different accounts, all with equally diverse axes to grind, but suddenly in the middle of this political quagmire, there came the mindblowing picture of Christ walking on the water. I had been living with the Sunday School version, I had it etched in my head, the ritualistic Victorian artist's creation of Christ pulling Peter up from the Sea of Galilee. The man in grey Terylene trousers annihilated that one. What took its place was far more vital. The only thing for it was a cigarette. A female ordinand and I both sat in the Methodists' College, puffing madly, drawing in the implications of what we had both seen. A raging storm, a shrouded boat, no moonlight, a figure walking over the waves. We both believed he was actually aiming to meet them on the other side as was planned. They, his disciples, didn't realize who it was at first.

He would have passed if they had not cried out. I can't say what Gospel gave me that version. It was a combination of absorbing the detail. The man in the Terylene trousers kept bringing his fist into his palm, saying, 'Look at the detail. Look at the detail.'

Well, it's Friday night. The week is over. I handed in my church history essay this afternoon; if this one goes down the Swannee, I have a bloody good mind to jump in after it. The big question in the common room meeting was, should we, as a student body, subscribe to *Evangelical Now*? As a magazine, it's not a jump-up-and-down, free-flowing, intellectual, artistically directed piece of work. The best I can say for it is the letters page, one which struck me as having been posted from the dark side of the moon. 'Was Judas's kiss a real kiss?' Is this a sexual question or was it a metaphorical kiss? What is a metaphorical kiss? How did Judas kiss Christ? The last few questions are mine. *Evangelical Now* didn't answer the question either. The vote was fourteen in favour, thirteen against and fifteen abstentions. Not what one might call conclusive. I felt that we bought a point of view masquerading as a magazine. It was a beautiful piece of politics; the Arch-Evangelical, who has the neatest hair and the loudest brogues in the college, had caught the rest of us on the hop. He'd organized his own supporters and the opposition had been completely unprepared. It was clinically done. As a married man, I live off the premises. I am eternally grateful for that. I can get away, escape the political undercurrent. It's not easy living in. There's no escape, not so much from God—Doctor Satan does his best on all of us—but from relentless group theology. I can misbehave here, I'm free from the expectations of all of them.

Tomorrow is the last official lecture of term. I have a sort of rogue lecture on Friday morning but tomorrow it's all over bar the polite discussion. I am actually buggered. I've overcooked it but that's an unavoidable consequence of merrily throwing myself at everything. We have a charity football match against a team calling themselves The Devil on Saturday morning. They've all been sponsored to grow goatee beards and are going on children's television to publicly rubbish us at nine o'clock in the morning. I'm sure stranger things have happened but that one stumps me right at this moment. This afternoon, following a one-and-a-half-hour long sociological exposition of rural life in Britain, those of us who had plumped for a 'rural PSU' duly received our briefing. PSU is college slang for Pastoral Study Unit. These are potentially very interesting and we all have to do at least one. The choice is staggering: you can join the Navy, become a Samaritan, learn about bereavement counselling, do hospital and hospice visiting, become attached to a secondary or primary school, join a media workshop or muck out cows and so on. The idea is to reflect theologically on experience gained in the field. So, eight of us humming with the dizzy expectations of chasing chickens for a week gathered to hear the received wisdom. It was all going very smoothly until a certain man sporting a dog collar explained that it was, in farming terms, usually a quiet week at the end of March. What was most worrying was that he had been a rural pastor all his life. He looked a trifle confused when someone pointed out that there is no such thing as a quiet week on a dairy farm, and when somebody else reminded him that this was traditionally the time of year when farmers were up all hours of the night with lambing, he stared at his leather shoes. Oh well, I can only assume he's been plodding the turf of some intensive grain-basket community for his long years of service.

They all look the same, vicars who've been at it for a while: watery eyes, strange Peruvian shoes and regulation grey trousers. They have the eyes of people who have seen more than enough. We may all go in different, but it's slightly worrying and in some ways reassuring that we may come out drifting more towards uniformity. Who knows, if I make retirement, will my eyes be watery? Will I have a large nose and obscure South American footwear? Even more worrying was that the Poacher said they all looked like his father. So they must put something in the wafer bread.

My DDO came to see me today. A DDO is a Diocesan Director of Ordinands. He's the person you see first of all if you think you are being called by God to become a minister. I'm sure he was Sweet Gene Vincent in his younger days; you know, black hair going grey, black jacket, dark tie, white shirt, black trousers, black shoes, black socks, all covered up by a black coat. I always try not to be impressed by these people. It's a losing battle. All the ones I have met drip empathy, you simply want to sit down and tell them absolutely everything: the good, the bad and the ugly. Their job is to establish whether or not you have a genuine calling. I would imagine there are certain pointers, but I would also think that each calling is completely unique and earthed through the individual concerned. We discuss our callings, not the nitty gritty: it's a great shame. Our calling is referred to as being a great source of strength when everything else fails. We're told to bear it in mind.

My calling started when I was about eighteen/nineteen: for no explainable reason I can think of, I simply felt I had to be a vicar. The picture was very clear in my mind. It felt, in one sense, overwhelming, almost physical, like waves passing through my body; and in another sense the most natural thing in the world. It was never frightening, there were no flashing lights, and it stayed with me for ten years. I couldn't shake it. Believe you me, I tried. It's easy to look back in a fervour of post-rationalization and claim, with the light in your eyes, that you can see God's hand nudging you this way and that, I can. I don't regard it as extraordinary, though it has always been beautiful, it has always been gentle, it has always been patient and it has always been loving and I have fought it tooth and bloody nail. I can't tell you what it feels like to have lost, only that in the losing, you truly find that God and you are found by Him, it is a meeting, and my wretched humanity, racked with wasteful pride, vice and selfishness, can only be of worth through that God. You don't have to have a stereotypical relationship, you can have your relationship and only you can have it. There was an excellent sermon last night. Graham Greene wrote this sentence. 'He became aware he missed happiness by seconds'. Like the man said, we've all done it and we'll all go on doing it. Tomorrow is the big game against the Devil.

Three-nil. What a result. They all appeared outside the college wearing red devil's horns and fake goatee beards. I think we won by default actually. They'd all been up bopping the night away in a Maidstone disco. Hardly bears thinking about. They then went on television, announced the game to the nation, jumped into a minibus and we were at the playing field by eleven forty-five.

This is the last week. Everyone seems a little too ragged around the edges to be demob happy, and it appears to be a time of reflection and last-minute essay writing. For some unknown reason Mad Dog has persuaded me to become the other half of the Blues Brothers in the Christmas review. The plan is to dress up in cassocks and dark glasses and sing a truly rotten version of Pink Floyd's 'Money' and a rewritten version of 'Alice's Restaurant', which has now become 'Muriel's Restaurant'. I can't say it's going to be the best fun I've ever had. In fact, I may wear a thick red balaclava as well.

The Last Day of Term

There was one essay that wasn't finished, 'What positive concern is shown for the nations by the New Testament writers and how do they do it?' It wasn't an easy question. I spent the whole day buried in books. The carol service was, I think, a great success. Mad Dog had roped me into this playlet about Mary and Joseph coming into the temple with the infant Jesus. I had seconded the Principal's wife as Simeon's wife. So, there we sat, beneath the altar in the half-light, reading this modern version with occasional characters jumping up from the congregation adding to the dialogue. The service was spiced with an overhead projector sliding images of Amazonian poverty at us all culminating in a family snapshot of an Indian couple holding their one minute old baby. This seasonal spectacular was brought to a climax by Slade blasting 'Merry Christmas Everybody', accompanied by balloons and jumping children. Halfway through dinner a fellow ordinand leant over and asked me, had I any idea what the play was about? I hadn't. After five days of reading it I'm still none the wiser. The meal was jolly. We did manage to let our hair down. We nearly had a food fight as well. I was definitely on for it. There were table mats and fir-cones flying everywhere. The old art of looking innocent having just launched a counter offensive with a mixture of table decorations and plum pudding: yes, yes! There were no winners, although Poacher claimed a victory of sorts when a double whammy of table mats caught me square on the nose. It died down when the Head of Academic Studies made it known that the person who had thrown a fir-cone into his coffee would meet a particularly un-Christian end. I think it was the two cans of Kestrel Super Strength that was my ultimate undoing. I had been rehearsing 'Money' by Pink Floyd, with a few choice word changes, and was dressed up with Mad Dog in a borrowed cassock, a pork-pie hat and a pair of wrap-around mirrored sunglasses, when I realized that I had run out of cigarettes. So, I went to the pub to buy some. Yes, I had a quick half and yes, I was dreading it because it was awful, but I was surprised to find half the college looking for me on my return. The show was over. It had finished at half past ten. I thought it was going on a lot longer. Anyway, the long and the short of it was that I had missed it. So, they'll just have to look forward to a fully-blown version in four weeks' time. I'm not sure that anything seems real yet, much of me is just going along with it all, there is the occasional moment where the experience seems solid enough, where what is happening appears to have purpose, but most of us are simply riding the wave with no idea where it's going.

January 1993

Christmas was madness. The house was crammed with people. A couple of days before the beginning of term two, I was asked for mulled cider at a fellow ordinand's home. Having been surrounded by unabashed atheists and Buddhists at Christmas, I was suddenly confronted with polite, considerate, 'Pass the Twiglets, please' reality. At about half past nine a game called Therapy was dropped in the middle of the carpet. I made my excuses.

To be honest, the first day back was rather wet and depressing. There were the usual announcements of meals, timetable changes and introductions of new faces. The Principal tried to liven the proceedings up with a decree that we were all to be encouraged to meet with the Holy Spirit at morning prayers, but no one appeared glad. It was a strange day.

Today, however, was a completely different story. At nine-thirty sharp, twenty-five of us from the Federation sat down with nervous smiles and our arms folded and embarked upon the 'Sexuality and Relationships' short course. This seemed to ignite the fuse, uncomfortable confrontations being better for the soul perhaps. We all introduced ourselves with some short anecdote on exactly why we were called what we were and why James was never Jim, and Andrew was only the name used by his wife when there'd been an argument. We then took an hour to work out a confidentiality agreement so that nothing of a personal nature could be used to blackmail future bishops—not that any of us have admitted anything remotely scandalous so far. We all then had to describe our ideal breakfast: where and who with. The scores were: Michelle Pfeiffer 4; Greta Scaatchi 2; Sean Connery 1, and wives and friends also popped up for the occasional extravaganza in Italy, the Caribbean or an Alpine coffee bar (you know, the one in the Martini ads).

The afternoon became a little more juicy. Two pieces of paper were placed on the floor. One said, 'Agree', and the other, 'Disagree'. The first proposal was, 'The choice is either marriage or celibacy'. The idea was then to stand either in the middle or, if you had a confirmed opinion, on one of the pieces of paper. I have to say, I made for the disagree spot. It was only when I was standing there I realized that I was the sole representative from my college with this particular view. We were then asked to explain our views to those who agreed with us and, having done that, to expound on our decision to those who disagreed. I was, I have to say, a tad more circumspect on the masturbation question that followed.

We were then split into smaller groups and asked to draw diagrams of what was acceptable sexual behaviour to us, sexual behaviour that we would tolerate but not practise and finally what, sexually speaking, was unacceptable. These views we shared with one other person. It was a brilliant day. It's refreshing to know that you can discuss anything when you want. Another two days of Sexuality and Relationships. I must clean my teeth.

Day two and three of the Sexuality and Relationships course didn't really have the same bite as day one. Not that what we learned wasn't fundamentally useful, necessary and, above all, relevant. It's just that we'd all grown accustomed to such words as transsexual and love-bites.

We were able to discuss our fears, our hang-ups and our weaknesses but this was done in twos. Most of all, I felt it taught all of us that our sexuality was as much a part of us as our appetite, and we should not be frightened of it. The proceedings on day three ended with deep division over the question of sex before marriage. It was on the point of becoming loud when the sexologists stepped in to separate the sparring partners. I can't believe I've just written 'the sexologists stepped in to separate the sparring partners'. Anyway, what it did prove was that there are serious differences over this issue. To my mind it was the discussion we should have had in a padded cell. We did need, all of us, to reflect on the implications of faith from what we had heard. Sadly, I feel, nobody budged an inch. I still can't help thinking that there are far more pressing questions Christians need to deal with than virginity.

The second course, before lectures began, I had plumped for was Church Management. For some as yet unknown reason, I was lucky enough to be doing both my first choices for course seminars. Most other ordinands were not. I can only assume it was the luck of the draw or that because I'm only here for two years, they feel that's reason enough for some positive discrimination.

I wish I could report that the Church Management day had been riveting. It is a hard job making the internal workings of a box file something to get excited about but I have to say, after five minutes on how to deliver church notices, my mind was wandering back to those heady days of the Sexuality and Relationships seminar. He was very serious at the end though, telling those of us who had endured the rigours of desk surface management, filing systems, correspondence correctness, the different uses of the telephone and generally how to order our unendingly cluttered lives, that the most important thing was time off and our families. However consuming the job might be, if we could discipline ourselves, every morning in our studies, to dealing with what needs to be dealt with there and then, our ministries would be better for it. I have to say, I intend to do just that.

I've spent the rest of the week between preparing a seminar on the remarkable Charles Simeon, darling of the Evangelicals—a colourful and rigorously faithful man—and the ill wind of crisis. It's been brewing since we returned. I can't really keep this up for much longer, this mirage that I am holy or that I even might be. There are some people here that most definitely smile with God. I don't—my cigarettes smoke loudly. In short, I reached the immensely boring conclusion that I'm not the same as them and, worst of all, I can't pretend I am for any longer.

It all came to a head on Saturday. I was waiting for my wife outside a shop when a college couple walked past. They hadn't seen me, I hadn't seen them, not until we were almost nose to nose. I adopted my usual tactful as a flying mallet approach and said 'Wotcha guys!' Their reaction was to: a) look horrified; b) put their heads down; c) stop holding hands. It isn't a new relationship. It's been going on since the beginning of last term. So why did they react that way? What is wrong with holding hands? Would God disapprove so much of Christians showing public affection for each other? I don't think so, not my God. He wouldn't mind, not if it was real. So why don't they think it is? It looked it to me. We have Christian couples announcing their engagement after 'going out' for eight and a half days. Now, I have no doubt that thunderbolt love strikes, but eight and a half days into a relationship is not the best time to dive into marriage. As Christians we don't have the ability to define love, to put barriers round it and call it names, to give it rules that constrict its growth. How can we allow our arrogance to do that? It is the one divine gift we all share. If we define it, we take something from it. We put it in a box and call it ours and make it small. And here it was, this defining act ending with a breaking of hands. Call me naive, but it wasn't a pretty sight. I poured all this out to my pastoral tutor over a beer; it's bloody religion, that's all it is.

I scrambled the church history seminar together on one Charles Simeon and the Evangelical revival of the Church of England in the late eighteenth and early nineteenth centuries. What a man: disciplined, courageous, vain, fastidious, immensely generous. He had fifty-seven years in one parish. He started the Sunday School Movement, was a prime mover in the Church Pastoral Aid Society, the British and Foreign Bible Society and several other notable organizations. Anyway, it was good to have done it. Bart and I sat down yesterday and worked out that we have one internal New Testament essay, one Old Testament exegesis, one New Testament seminar and, once those are done, between six and seven external essays which have a deadline of 17 May. External essays have to be between three and five thousand words. Internal work is generally somewhere around three thousand words. The next milestone is an external sociology essay on the relationship between the church and the secular press that needs to be handed in three weeks from now. Mucho worko!

I'm still on the edge of crisis. It really feels like all my anchor chains have been cut and that the boat is being buffeted from one large wave to another. It's an extremely uncomfortable experience. I am determined to use these two years as a chance to listen to all views, and experience God and Christ as espoused by fickle humanity in all its colours, prejudices and varying degrees of polyester and Terylene. I'm determined my view should be challenged right down to the wire. I did not come here to have myself confirmed as a Christian, I came here knowing that I would have to lose everything, that everything would have to be thrown into the air. Well, I've just about lost sight of it. I almost don't expect to see any of it again. It's a process that takes place deep inside you. You would have to be either very sure or very stupid for the study of others' opinions, for the whole experience of theological college, not to hit you right in the guts where, frankly, it bloody well hurts.

After the obligatory session with my pastoral tutor he handed me a form for my self-assessment. I have just counted forty-seven or so questions that we're encouraged to consider on two sides of A4. I still can't understand why everyone gets into such a tizz about these reports to your bishop. Sure, he wants to know how the person is getting on but I really don't see it as a big deal. Apparently they cause huge amounts of wailing and gnashing of teeth. Maybe when the Principal reads mine to me, I'll get the picture.

Last night about twenty of us started a bereavement counselling course. It wasn't harrowing, it was sobering. We all sat there looking up occasionally, catching each other's eyes, all thinking, 'I'm not going to be able to do this. I'm not going down to a hospital mortuary with a young woman to help her identify her husband and eleven-year-old son who have been mutilated in a car crash.' Some of us as ministers are going to have to face situations like that.

Football this afternoon. If we don't win two of our remaining four games, we will be relegated to the third division. Come on you curates, come on you curates!

Well, it's been an abyss of a day. James Cameron has just stunned my senses with his exquisite exposition on life at the bottom of the ocean and molecular water control. But, before that, Edmond, a Franciscan monk, hit me right in the teeth. I've asked him to be my spiritual director. A spiritual director is someone who gardens your soul, points out the weeds and waters the roses. The Franciscans are, in my opinion, God's SAS. For my church attachment, I persuaded my pastoral tutor that that's where things would be most fruitful for me. The reply to my question of 'Would you be my spiritual director?' was, 'I'm in a state of flux. I think God is asking me to be a tramp.' Now, you of little faith can have a good old giggle at the apparent insanity of it all. I, on the other hand, can honestly think of nothing more than: here we go, here we go. Edmond and I have the same God. Those were the first words I have heard here that set fire to my brain. To go with no direction other than the Lord's is stupid, pitiful and utterly, utterly beautiful. The nature of ministry in churches had been bothering this wretched spirit increasingly. Our idea of priests is, by and large, as conservative as most of them undoubtedly are. This, for me, is what the Holy Spirit is all about. For others it will be different.

Political life has also increased in temperature with the imminent resignation of the Archdeacon. The Archdeacon is, in fact, the senior ordinand, all very hierarchical stuff, and it's their job to convey the whines and worries and general observations of the common room to the staff and, most notably, the Principal. The logistics of this really revolve around committees. So, knowing that a great deal of time is spent organizing meeting dates and less time is spent actually having meetings, the Archdeacon hasn't been overwhelming in his praise for the job and, if you look the slightest bit sensible, he sort of lets it be known that only a complete idiot would want to have anything to do with it. I know Poacher hasn't said anything but he would be good. Everybody loves him except himself. The tactics are not to reveal your hand until just before the closing date for nominations, in that way it's possible to avoid lorry loads of gossip that's bound to spring from someone with obvious and now entirely open megalomaniac tendencies. I'm considering it seriously but I think, with a baby coming, hopefully in August, it is little more than wishful thinking. There's a lot of hideously polite jockeying for positions though, as this obvious recognition of popularity goes down in your report to your sponsoring diocese. Sponsoring dioceses are the ones that fork out the readies for ordinands to attend theological college. It must have been a system devised by Al Capone.

Each diocese behaves differently: some fall over themselves to help ordinands; others, in my opinion, behave very badly indeed, specifying how many children you're allowed to have while you are attending college, and enforcing wives without children to work. This is odious in the extreme and one should not be bullied or dictated to in any sense. Living on a grant and going through the process of training is hard enough without having to conform to a list of officious and contentious dictates. I have nothing but praise for my diocese. They have been sympathetic, helpful, realistic and ready to listen. I'm only sorry for those people who have had a different experience and there are far too many of them.

February 1993

Me back's gone. I saw the doctor: he said it's just a strain to go with the other ones. The sociology essay has gone down the tubes. This isn't quite as bad as it sounds, it just means that I'll have an extra essay to do next year. The good news, however, is that I passed my second Old Testament essay: quick pirouette. All that's left is an exegesis and an external essay. My policy of cramming everything into the beginning of term is not working the wonders it was intended to. I may well have overcooked it on that front. I am very tired and it is my own fault entirely. Celtic Christianity has lived up to all my expectations. Every Monday we dive into the world of monks and far away places. Before the Roman way of doing religion barged its way in here, we were, it appears, managing quite well thank you without it. Everything changed at the Council of Whitby back in the Dark Ages and, although we're in danger of not seeing the reality for the stars in our eyes, it does appear, from reading the poetry and the prayers, that our distant forefathers, who didn't have to grapple with Fundamentalists' disapproval, Evangelical blindness and Charismatic excesses, had a more earthy approach to their loving and gentle God. Anyone who can live in an isolated stone hut off the southwest coast of Ireland and eat fish for breakfast, lunch and supper for years on end gets my vote.

Speaking of food, it seems the meal credit system is collapsing under its own popularity. How's this for logic? The system, we've all been told, is designed around a 70 per cent take-up factor. What that means is that, having lovingly filled in the meal quota form, it's assumed that you'll only eat 70 per cent of the meals. What's happening is that we're all eating 100 per cent of our meals. I have a feeling that such calculated optimism could only be based on faith or, more sinister still, this is a calculated political precursor to a 30 per cent cut in food. Who can say?

The weather here is wintery, barren; the skies are colourless, drawing grave tones from the bricks and trees, bending the bodies of those walking in the wild wind. Feelings are running high with the partners who are complaining they never see their other halves. I'm not sure that this is actually fair. I think we perhaps see more of our partners—the problem is one of quality time. I work every evening and the evening I don't work I'm doing a counselling course or I'm at a service of some kind. The Church of England operates a six-day week, vicars only have one day off. From what I can gather they are at work when the rest of the population isn't; this not only completely screws up their social life but also puts quite a strain on their marriages. The weekends we used to have as a family simply do not exist any more; the idea of doing all the domestic necessities on a Saturday and relaxing on Sunday is an impossibility for vicars. Marriages are under even more pressure if the partner works which they increasingly do out of financial necessity. I'm not complaining about the hours we do, most professional people in secular employment work just as hard, the difference is they have the rewards in terms of time, money and leisure. We don't and it's this I believe that ultimately defeats individuals and marriages. The pressure is relentless on all sides. There's never any let up. My mind is fundamentally clear on this, my marriage and my family come first and I will not sacrifice them for the church.

I finally snapped in the rehearsals for tomorrow's Gregorian chant. Sixteenth-century eulogism is essentially meaningless and irrelevant at the best of times; set to music it becomes nothing more than an exercise in self-gratification. So, I'm afraid I left. It's no good making excuses. Do they speak like that in heaven? Did Christ speak in sixteenth-century English to Peter, to James, to John? So why do we persist with this madness? Today we had a communications lady come in and explain about posture and diction so that when we are finally let loose, people may understand what we're trying to explain and we may understand a little more in how to communicate our messages properly. In descending order, it goes like this: people take in your actions first, in a sense we are a reflection of how we feel, nervous, irritable, charming, open, whatever (very interesting that Adolf Hitler must have been very charming at some stage); then we are judged on how we look, smart, scruffy, angelic, rip-roaringly cool; and finally, a paltry seven per cent of what we say is remembered, that's all. I put this to Poacher who'd bunked the session. He looked up at me ruefully from behind an untidy pile of books and said that 7 per cent from 100 per cent quality was not to be sniffed at. Do we only have 7 per cent of what Christ said? Considerably less, I would imagine.

That apostle Paul, I have come to the conclusion, judging people on all three, must have been a funny mixture. He wrote beautifully, persuasively, forcefully. He set up many churches, from Rome to Macedonia. So, what did he look like then, this Pharisee that saw the light? How was his face proportioned? The bottom line is, would you like him as your vicar or your pastoral tutor? Most people say no. Possibly because there doesn't appear as yet to be anything beyond him. He's so large, so dominating, so intimidating. Maybe the reason he travelled round so much was that people could only stand a month of his company, who knows?

The 'sound' boys are definitely taking over. These are the 'bible for a brain' Conservative Evangelicals. They dress smartly, they don't come to any of the organized social sessions, they eat together, go on missions together, and laugh at the same jokes. Their leader is the Arch-Evangelical whose mission in life is to submit the population of the world to scripture and the heady delights of beagling.

It must have been the full packet of candy sticks that really disagreed with my constitution. There's something very humbling about sitting on the loo at half past three in the morning with your head in a bucket. Anyway, no more candy sticks. Sadly, it meant that I missed the stunning 3–2 victory in football and a church history lecture on the church's response to Darwinism, which was a pity. I was looking forward to both. However, the enforced convalescence meant I was able to squeeze more than usual out of 1 Thessalonians for a New Testament seminar yesterday. It's rather worrying how quickly you get used to delivering seminars. They are meant to be in place of essays. However, I have to say that they require a lot less work.

The rave service was not a rip-roaring, let's get down and boogie success. We all piled into the lecture room which had been transformed into what appeared to be the internal organs of the Starship Enterprise. Every corner was regurgitating wires and there was a complicated construction of platforms and boxes, projectors and screens. The music oozed heavenly choirs out of two large speakers which sat on top of the library shelves. Why we all sat on chairs, I don't know. All this would have been fine, except I couldn't help thinking that what 'rave services' needed was a 'rave' vicar, not the model 1936 version that presided over the occasion. I'm sure I caught him, at least once, wincing in the shadows above a large screen that read 'Rescue me' in huge letters. Very few of us were carried away by the throbbing music; there were one or two who bobbed up and down like a yo-yo stuck to the floor, but no great outpouring of emotion and verve. Most people looked confused, culturally displaced, as the three television screens aimed images of waste and destruction encompassing everything from napalm to take-away beefburgers; from among the words fired in quick succession from the screens, I did manage to glean the sentence 'The media is the antichrist', but I couldn't keep up after that: was the Holy Spirit with us? Yes, but we couldn't have known it, we were all far too busy swallowing the imagery, hearing the rhythm. Also, it didn't quite get there. The whole thing was based on a Eucharist and, as much as I admire the Alternative Service Book, it really wasn't quite up to being pronounced by an eminent, ageing Australian vicar over the strains of techno-rap. The whole effect ultimately resembled the B-side of a minor Seventies hit. But what potential. We've all got to start somewhere. It could have been brilliant. What it really could have done with was Jim Morrison but you need a rock-and-roll heart for that stuff.

Fittingly, the Egomaniacs won the quiz that followed and a bottle of Bulgarian red. Our team came second and had to settle for Austrian Liebfraumilch which I can't say anyone looked particularly eager to drink. This weekend is a retreat prayer weekend, so I'm leaving home for two days of prayer in the wilds.

Well, we did the customary things: the introduction circle where we all said a few words about ourselves, we said grace and watched the rugby and prayed a lot. Prayer is the magical essence of Christianity, the presence of the Holy Spirit within us. I'm not sure whether it's teachable. Most people have the one experience in common, and that is, when your prayer life goes everything else tends to come toppling down around it. The house was a typical Christian establishment; ordered, clean. There were discreet corners with varying degrees of kitsch pictures placed inside them. The carpets were grey. The chairs were uncomfortable. The food was unremarkable. I had a lovely room overlooking the garden. It was about the size of a small bathroom but it was warm.

There is still a lot of tension, corporate tension. The problem seems to be competition. We are all after all in competition with each other or will be. I hate it because it's destructive and divisive. Everything you do, everything you are, seems to allude to your own personal relationship with God. It's always going to be different; not better, not worse, just different. To cram all that into a box and call it right or wrong is a big mistake. I'm naive enough to believe we are equal before God. I wish there was more to say, that the wind of the Holy Spirit blew strong in our hearts. I don't feel it did.

My supervision with the elocution lady was far more vibrant. She was one of those Jaeger-dressed immaculate mothers with a smattering of artistic darling thrown in for good measure. She liked my rendition of the sixteenth-century chant attacking the use of the Book of Common Prayer. She enthralled that it was awfully good but not quite Radio Four. She thought I had a lovely voice but that I might vary my inflection somewhat more ruthlessly. She again suggested that anyone who had a seat on Synod had to have a very strong faith because taking part in Synod, and this appears to be the general consensus, is usually enough to encourage most people to embrace Hare Krishna. That, to me, reads like slimy back-stabbing politics, integral power games and arrogant pomp, all cloaked in polite smiles and erudite etiquette. Sounds great. I would imagine it's rather like theological college, the in-fighting and all that cloak and dagger dancing, the whispers behind closed doors and theological alliances.

March 1993

Taking morning prayers is a daunting experience. You're aware that every inflection is being scrutinized, every pose observed. It's a hostile congregation, even at a quarter past eight in the morning. I think it went OK. We sang 'Be Thou My Vision' and read the Benedictus and Psalm 10. I find I'm actually aware of language, the language we use. I know there have been concerted attempts to make what we say inclusive. However, I'm not completely convinced that this has not added to the exclusive nature of everything that is said in churches. Certainly the BCP, however beautiful, however Shakespearean, is irrelevant to the way we speak today. I know it's a fraught debate.

We lost the football 8–3 even though we played like men possessed. Our goalie didn't particularly keep morale up by yelling, 'We can still win this one, lads,' every time the opposition scored. But it was a fine game although we are now out of the cup. We've just started on Jesus in New Testament studies. It promises to be mind-blowing.

It is: actually to dive critically into the life and mission of Christ is nothing less than an extraordinary event. He is so deep within the consciousness of the world, our lives; all our lives have been touched by this man whether we like it or not. We are living in his time, it's his calendar, our weeks still revolve very much around an acknowledgment of his presence on Earth. The villages and towns here in this country echo to his presence, it's etched across the ages in every churchyard, Chapel, cathedral and mission hall, his song left in the resonance of the ringing bells, whispered on the lips of lovers and caught in the last-breath amen. The most remarkable thing is that we know so little about him. We can discern clues from the Gospels, adapt theories, piece his character together from his words, but all of this I view as essentially unreliable secondhand evidence, loaded with a hidden agenda of some kind. Yet, through all that ducking and diving of humanity, he still comes through burning the pages, scorching our consciousness.

Today we looked at what is meant by the 'Kingdom' that Jesus speaks about. Before that we indulged ourselves in an hour-long session on 'What is meant by preaching?' Preaching has had some very bad press of late: dictatorial, imperialistic, dogmatic. I agree with all those. However, they only serve to demonstrate that it's not preaching that's a lifeless excuse to think about lunch, but that the preachers themselves have bread sauce on the brain. The lecturer informed us he averaged an hour's work for every minute preached, a fifteen-minute sermon taking fifteen hours to prepare. There is a saying that is, 'You can either be a preacher and nothing else or you can be a pastor and not a preacher.' I agree with the latter and it is probably the parish minister who has all those pressures who is unable to dedicate as much time as he/she would like to preaching. It's a fact of life, we perhaps need to be more ruthless in managing it.

I was struck this morning on how little hair ordinands have. Poacher is definitely losing it on top, but even if you leave out those whom mother nature has taken a thinning comb to, there's hardly a sideburn in sight. There are two moustaches and three beards out of sixty-five people. I'm seriously considering taking the Celtic tonsure. I'm not convinced that anyone would notice. By and large most of us have disappeared inside ourselves. We're less rowdy, more reflective. The pressure of work is intense. It takes everything from you, bleeds you of anything impulsive. Bart has clearly been down this road before, his mind is tuned to the demands of the academic rhythm, he knows the rules, I don't. He is a genuinely decent man—I like him more and more. At first I thought sharing a study with him was going to be a disaster but it's been quite the reverse. I would trust my life with Bart. I don't think I have ever met a man with so much integrity. He will be a quite amazing priest.

The publicity committee whose job it was to sing the praises of all the theological colleges in this city didn't look altogether promising. I'd volunteered for it when I arrived and this was its first official get together. For a start it was the colour of limitless variations of khaki and following on from the ruthless ordering by the man in glasses on the church administration course, we made every mistake in the book.

1) There was no agenda.
2) There was no time limit.
3) The members of the committee had no idea of the subject matter the committee had been convened to discuss.

We sat in a cold room, for the most part listening to each other breathing. After one minute in, it all became painfully clear and the option of incarcerating myself in the Methodists' freezer which, for some reason probably only known to a handful of trusted Methodists, appeared to have been left in the lecture room we were meeting in, looked more and more appealing. Finally, an hour or so after not deciding that the new brochure should be black, orange, etched or photographed and some deft political jockeying, the decision was to make our proposals to the standing committee and, if they approved them, up to the full committee. What worries me most is that these committees have about as much knowledge of PR and graphics as a carrot does of the Song of Solomon.

This evening's counselling course was illuminating. I was just on the point of thinking what an immensely valuable two hours this had been when our tutor, who was summing up earnestly, suggested that we should 'expose ourselves to as many people as possible'. I tried my best to restrain myself but it was no use, I lost it completely. Poacher did his best to salvage my crumbling credibility by coughing loudly and suggesting that 'it wasn't that type of exposing' but that really made matters worse. We also lost the football 2–1. We missed a penalty. However, we've managed by the skin of our teeth to avoid relegation so we must hope for better things next season. There's one more match remaining and then we have the delights of the Methodist college's football tournament.

The tat deacon invited a Newcastle firm of clerical repute to display their wares in the common room after lunch today. Cassocks of all shape and colour and size were hung high on movable rails. They're not cheap. I suppose it's supply and demand. We're talking one hundred and sixty pounds here and that's before a surplus, shirts and any extra bits you might fancy. I don't have a cassock. I'm still slightly concerned about all this black, it's very dour. I finally plumped, having spent half an hour putting my head where the arms should be, for a thirty-nine-button number. It was the only one that my wife could look at without saying I resembled a marquee that needed the Samaritans or a hamster that had got lost in a napkin. Once again, there are rules. A double-breasted bit there and a button here all mean that you're of the Anglo-Catholic, Evangelical or monastic persuasion. What is important are shoes. Your congregation will definitely be able to see your shoes and doubtless judge you accordingly. I'm not completely convinced about all these expensive dressing gowns. I have a sneaking suspicion they paint all the wrong images about God; is God really grand? A study in ermine and silk? The real problem perhaps is that they make us different. I'm not sure we are and if we are it should be because of who and what we are and not what we wear.

The preaching course started in earnest today: there were all these marvellous titles and quotes from one Charles Simeon on the dos and don'ts of inspiring the congregation to learning and fervour. This instruction came with a list of books, a whole wood's worth on preaching technique. The most distressing thing is looking back on the countless sermons I've heard since I've been here. I honestly only remember one, that's it—he huffed and puffed a lot—the rest of them fall into the vague category. The thought of having to stand up every Sunday and hit them, wallop, right between the eyes, is a daunting one. Here we are, living the excesses of the techno age, where big babies spend billions persuading us their products are kind to kittens and lovely on your skin and yet, with very little support, every Sunday a parish priest holds forth on Christ, God, Ezekiel and Romans 8. We're meant to do it brilliantly of course. That's after a week of marriage preparation, baptism classes and the rest of it. Maybe we should specialize: the brilliant preachers preaching, the brilliant pastors pastoring.

The Sunday Times kicked off yesterday morning with the depressing headline 'Carey Catastrophe'. It was a vitriolic piece citing the closure of theological colleges, the lack of leadership and the financial crisis eating away at the Church of England. Someone managed to lose a cool half a billion on the property market. It's difficult to escape from the feeling of joining an underprivileged, underpaid minority group where the light at the end of the tunnel has been switched off. It's the old chestnut. Apparently, the Church of England has never been perfect. There was a period at the beginning of this century when, for a moment, every single parish that was meant to have a vicar had one but, by and large, we've apparently stumbled along on a cartload of compromise and polite but deadly politics. However, there is sadly an undercurrent of consensus that we are running out of petrol and that the Archbishop of Canterbury is steering without the wheel attached to the car. It can become very demoralizing knowing that the organization you are joining is lost in the labyrinth of commercial mind games. There simply doesn't seem to be the will to do anything properly.

I have precisely seven more essays to do before 17 May, five of those have to be more than three thousand words each.

One down, six to go. The Pauline essay on the New Testament course is sitting neatly on the table. I'm going to hit Isaiah very hard next week. We lost the football 8–5. We were in fact 2–0 up after ten minutes, at which point I think the opposition's charity ran out. It was a dirty game. If you can imagine a referee out of the Bash Street Kids, the typical cartoon referee, a cross between Hitler and Blakey from 'On the Buses', well, we had him for the first half. He was blind, deaf and had the knobbliest knees I'd ever seen, and where did he find those baggy Fifties soccer shorts?

Every Thursday, one student has to produce an expository thought for morning prayers to last no longer than three minutes. Invariably they ramble on to about ten. Yesterday's was particularly brilliant. It was all about Sodom and

Gomorrah, the angels cast as strangers, relating to our treatment and society's treatment of the strangers in our midst. We're on a fast today: no breakfast and no lunch. I'm afraid I sneaked a biscuit at about twelve and then, realizing that I'd failed, tucked in to a bacon and tomato sandwich.

I had a very charming letter from the Bish, congratulating all present for the forthcoming baby. He had beautiful writing, it wasn't typed, and signed; he hand-wrote the whole thing. It was very impressive.

Pastoral tutors like to visit you at home once during the year. It was us last night. I was particularly weary, having cooked a Lamb Diopaiza for the curry club the night before. I tell you, twenty-six popadoms disappeared down eight mouths in the time it took me to walk to the cooker. After his third glass of Bailey's my tutor tabled an informal motion to put off any prospective candidates for next year's places who arrived sporting a spectacular lack of style.

The community evening bit the dust at morning prayers. Reactions against it from those who were present were deeply hostile. If you think, in any one week we have seven compulsory services and one on Sunday. Our suggestion was to make morning prayers optional on the days we have a Eucharist. I don't think they will buy it. The problem is, we simply don't spend enough time together to generate a feeling of 'community' which is what I would imagine the Bishop's inspectors must have sensed for them to have suggested it. They've missed the point completely though: if they had really wanted to engender a sense of community they might have suggested we have fewer compulsory events, not more. What's most worrying is this contentious edict sadly demonstrates a spectacular lack of imagination and understanding.

The guest-night dinner didn't really set fire to the social senses either. Guest-night dinners are really a way of thanking all those responsible for taking ordinands into a parish church environment, mainly parish vicars and a rag-bag of ecclesiastical luminaries. They all turned up dressed in various shades of black, apart from two Franciscan monks who looked roaringly conspicuous in brown cassocks. My spiritual director, one of the Franciscan monks, downed a glass of sherry in just about one almighty sip. Watching the guests file in awkwardly, I made a hasty exit for the college bar and gave a bottle of beer the Franciscan treatment. On my return, the common room was filled to capacity with smartly dressed students surrounded by men in black. It resembled a wake for an undertaker. Mad Dog was there, his hair greased back; he's been working very hard lately locked away in his study for hours; his skin is the colour of weak wallpaper paste. He looked like a cross between Ronnie Kray and a ghost. He told me how he used to take off to Israel and wander the desert on his own and I didn't know he had volunteered himself for the reserve preaching rota which means he spends most Sunday mornings thumping the pulpit in a collection of churches he has never been to; a man indeed of hidden depths.

This week, the church history class witnessed the last lecture of the retiring Australian British Church History lecturer. He was a very fine lecturer. I wish I'd had him at ten years old. We clapped him out, his head bowed. It was, in a sense, the close of another chapter of history. When he was an ordinand, the regime was far more self-assured: prayers in the morning, compulsory; prayers before lunch, compulsory; Matins, compulsory; compline, compulsory. They didn't have as much church history to learn and that probably explained the fact that I never saw him look at any liturgical book when he was taking a service. His briefcase will no doubt retire with him. I was almost expecting him to nonchalantly toss it into the crowd. Maybe he's saving it for a grand finale. Thank you Reverend Pollard, from one who has sat smothered in flies in the bush. You're a beauty.

The election of the Archdeacon has been done. It's all over. Following the traditional neurosis. The nomination form was still empty twenty minutes before the deadline for nominations. It had been up for the best part of a month. I nominated Poacher; he'd also been nobbled by half the college to stand. I didn't feel altogether good about it because earlier on in the year I had suggested to one of the female ordinands that she should go for it; this in fact turned out to be the only other nomination. In the event it went to Poacher. To celebrate, he wore probably one of the most revolting jackets I've ever seen in my life. In fact, the combination of a mustard-coloured jacket and an open-neck blue-and-green paisley shirt made his offer of a glass of Thunderbird wine look strangely appealing.

The counselling course this evening was somewhat tense. We were all primed as to the symptoms to look out for in schizoid, paranoid, neurotic and schizophrenic members of the public. I am so tired I've really nothing left in reserve. I'm also not spending enough time with my wife and my daughter. I resent that. My wife is working, we desperately need the money so our marriage is under a lot of strain. When the pressure is on I go inwards deep inside myself. My wife is the opposite: she needs to talk without the distractions that money brings; and of course moving to a new environment we have been thrown much closer together. It is changing the balance of our relationship; this isn't always easy.

It's all over for the lectures. I missed the last one. We have a few next term which is mysteriously called the Easter Term; it actually takes place in the summer. Well, I'm halfway through everything. It has been one of those weeks. This college is ruthlessly efficient. The fabulous Franciscan from my attachment church phoned because he had been sent a form to fill in and return, 'Would I help him with it?' He came over and we ended up discussing our culinary recollections of the guest-night dinner which centred around the toothpaste cheesecake. He then reluctantly took the form out of his pockets and we got down to business. Was I punctual? Did I show instinct? Was I popular, empathetic? What had I done? What hadn't I done? Why hadn't I done it? There was everything on there except my marmalade preference and whether I was kind to lonely gerbils. To be honest, it was all rather embarrassing, not the actual joint form-filling, more the necessity for the questions. It seemed to me to be one of those exercises that served absolutely no purpose whatsoever and it reeked of a report. Something somebody glanced at no more.

I missed the meeting but apparently was elected as social secretary. This didn't come as a great surprise; with no one actually standing against me the outcome was hardly in question. Several other posts were also filled for next year's power game. Bart is the new secretary, he'll do a blinding job I reckon, he has an excellent computer manner. The treasurer is the sort of man who if, by some unlikely chance, decided to bicycle across the Grand Canyon on a piece of fishing line would still inspire enough confidence to be entrusted with your entire savings to take across with him. The book deacon loves books and the food deacon likes fishing.

The big day was Thursday. We were all thrown into a seminar on the Green church. It all started amicably enough. A man with a very soft and sincere voice showed up and said that he was going to take us through the fine print of the Rio Earth Summit. On the way, we saw pictures of the Brazilian underground, pictures of the conference centre, pictures of the people he said hello to the night before and pictures of the famous Tree of Life conceived, we were told, by Jonathan Porrit. I'm afraid that's where I lost it. Here we face probably the most important issue of our times, the planet is dying, this gift to us from God, we're killing it and everything on it and in the meantime the Church of England is showing us pictures of the Brazilian underground. My theology on this issue is unbending. Despite Darwin's obvious brilliance, Stephen Hawking's raving genius and Einstein's beautiful theory we are, I believe, on God's earth. The theory of evolution only confirms that in my view we have been entrusted with the safe-keeping of this planet. If you love your neighbours, you do not steal from them, you do nothing at your neighbour's expense. That includes dropping litter, dumping sewage at sea, selling someone a ropy secondhand car or poisoning the rivers with nitrate fertilizers. It includes corporate destruction of the ozone layer and all. It has to stop. If you love God with all your heart, all your mind and strength, you are not going to piss in your neighbour's soup. It means that people picking the bananas that you eat are paid a fair and reasonable wage. Love your neighbour as yourself. Do unto others as you would have them do unto you.

There are no grey areas whatsoever. The tree of life was not Jonathan Porrit's idea; it emerged at a brainstorm in London which he attended along with about eight other people. If this is the Church of England's environmental expert, all he managed to achieve was to add considerably to the greenhouse effect; it was a tragic farce.

Studying theology is a monumental privilege. To look into the heart of humanity, attempting to discern the heart of God, obviously has its knock on effects. My sense of the Holy Spirit has been mushrooming ever since I arrived. The boundaries of the Holy Spirit have increased dramatically. It feels as if the Holy Spirit is really the glue that holds life together: the force, if you like. The Holy Spirit, to me, is love. It is a physical presence, quite discernible and recognizable. It is a presence that, I believe, is sensed by your whole being. It is at the heart of creation, creation grows in it, through it, from it. It is always a beautiful presence. It is the source of love. We are quite literally bathed in love. An awareness of the Holy Spirit explodes our own intellectual boundaries of what we perceive love to be.

On to the disco. The disco was a raving success. Yes, the amp packed in a couple of times due to the walloping volume forced through its knackered circuits. The Principal and I took it in turns to man the turntables and, I have to say, the crowd went apeshit. I even saw a pair of leopard-skin trousers and a leather jacket. The Principal also went to town on the dress front. He was wearing the widest pair of white loons I've seen since 1972, a very long paisley cravat and a kaftan jacket. The bar ran out of beer and Status Quo held court underpinning the arias of Deep Purple and Spirit in the Sky. The vicars danced. They danced very well albeit with each other. One more essay to go before the big ones.

The Easter Term

The flu. My temperature hovered interestingly just above one hundred and three for four days. By the time the Old Testament exegesis was handed in, I was wobbling intellectually as well as physically. So, here we are, back on the chain gang. *Was I in my study over the vac? Can I bowl or bat? Lectures are compulsory*, plus a myriad of other reminders. I'm never very comfortable at the beginning of term. It never quite seems to gel. I've completed my pastoral studies experience over the vacation with a week milking cows and applying theological insights into the

Wheatsheaf and several other hospitable rural community centres. Did anyone ever see the vicar? No. Was there a vicar? Yes. And that's really where the conversation ended, until they discovered this was all part of my training and insisted on calling me the 'Rev' for the following week. I have to say, the countryside was glorious. I don't want to disappear into Kebleisms, but it is God's garden and we are pulling out the flowers. Poacher's rural experience was somewhat less energetic than my own. He turned up in his dirtiest boots every morning, drank tea for an hour, lobbed a couple of bails over the side of a trailer, chased a couple of hares into hedges and was at home by 11 o'clock in the morning. So wearing his best ham grin he told me that he had whiled away the hours writing the mega 'pass or be damned' external essays. I have four to do, the examiners want between three thousand and five thousand words apiece. I'm doing one on the Anglo-Catholic Movement, one on 'Did Jesus expect an imminent end of the world?' and finally, I will attempt to tackle the thorny question of 'Was God a God of War?'

The reading is all but done for the Anglo-Catholic extravaganza. There are some seriously meaty issues to get stuck into on that front. Emotionally, it's a strong argument, very strong. Cardinal Newman, although apparently joyless, was obviously frighteningly clever. I would question Keble's attempts at poetry but at least he had a go. Along with the glories of the cowshed there was a mild flirtation with the press over the vac. I wrote an article for the *Evening Standard* on advertising and the church. My wife brought a copy home with her. There was a large mugshot of yours truly underneath a ruddy great headline which read 'HOLY UNSUITABLE'. Whether that was a reference to the picture or the subject matter was a question tantalizingly left open to the readership.

On the subject of reading, as a student one Cardinal Newman apparently managed to read nonstop for anything between twelve and sixteen hours a day, so with his academic athletics in mind I have installed a ruthless programme to carry me through these essays. Work, exercise, work, collect my daughter from nursery, then more work once she is in bed. My wife is working in London again so my daughter is coming to Chapel with me every morning. I have the Principal's permission to miss all afternoon and evening Eucharists. Yes, it's going to be a hell of a month. Here comes exercise.

May 1993

I've done it. Just under five thousand words on the changing character of the High-Church Party in the nineteenth century. I decided to tackle it because I have to say, I've never been one for dishing out the incense. However, I must say, it's blown my mind. The theory of an unbroken line of discipleship from Christ through to my own humble theological college is frightening indeed, awesome in fact. It raises issues which have been dragged through the flames over the debate for the ordination of women on who governs the Church: an essentially parliamentary-approved Synod or the Church? I have to say, looking at Norman Tebbit, I can see no good reasons for allowing the State to approve and sanction the appointment of bishops.

All those leaving next year had an hour's debrief on the complexities of securing a curacy. There was a strange sense of foreboding about the whole affair. For one thing, I don't even feel like I've really settled in yet and we're talking about leaving already. Secondly, the thought of having a boss doesn't appeal to me.

As a curate, you can choose, within reason, where you would like to go. It's a very vague reason and the differences are essentially this: rural or city. That's it. Securing a curacy, however, is very much more fraught with complexities.

All the dioceses of the Church of England have a different number of ordinands. Some have too many to fill their quota of curates, others do not have enough. This is where the horse trading starts. A diocese (the Bishop) has to release you from his group if he is unable to offer you a curacy from whence you came. In short, I've taken this to mean that your Bishop looks at your report and decides whether or not he wants anything further to do with you. If the answer is that he does, then you are offered a curacy, or perhaps two, in the diocese. If he doesn't, then you're in the basket. As an ordinand, you can circumvent these delicate politics by asking your diocese to release you (you have to ask them to release you because they have in fact been paying for your training). Once you've been released, the problems start.

A vicar who has been given a budget for a curate (that's me) is only allowed to see one candidate at a time. He/she is not allowed to line you up outside his study and choose the one with the most colourful leisure suit or whatever takes his fancy.

The ordinand, for their part, is only allowed to look at one parish at a time and is not encouraged to scout around, looking for the best house a parish has to offer that's hopefully no more than one hundred yards from the church. The situation is further complicated by the fact that a vicar looking for a curate on the open market receives CVs of prospective candidates so he/she can choose from those.

The system is, of course, unworkable because anyone with any sense is ignoring it. Those who are playing by the rules have a distinct disadvantage because of the networks that exist within the Church of England, which brings me back to my essay. Vicars of a High Church persuasion are hardly likely to view CVs from an Evangelical college with anything other than a spontaneous outpouring of sympathy. Why don't we all go to one theological college? The church clearly cannot afford to support the twelve or so that are left. So, they should sell them (they would make millions). Not only are there economies of scale here but we would have a decent football team and the extremes at the wings of persuasion would get to sit down and discuss their views over a shepherd's pie which brings me to my Old Testament question 'Was God a God of War?'

In the absence of a reading list, I actually plumped for a pastoral studies essay which took me into the wild waters of Green theology: 'Have we over-emphasized the redemption at the expense of creation?' It was a frightening exercise that essentially involved open-heart surgery on the Church of England. I spoke with several of our eminent Green theologians and a very erudite Catholic in Yorkshire. As the day progressed, a more depressing picture of vested interest, terminal mediocrity and some delicate dancing in the hierarchical minefield emerged.

There is no Green movement in the church. We have aligned ourselves, out of necessity I have no doubt, with the authority of the State. It seems our job is to marry, bury and bless on demand. Any variation on that, any rocking of the corporate boat, is not encouraged. Much like the secular world, rule one is don't stand out too much; it is the plodders that get there in the end. Very rarely do those with a stroke of genius make it, by and large, they tend to get very bored with the plodders and explode in spectacular fashion along the way, and the safe pair of hands that is invariably given the reins ultimately strangles everything and everybody. Anyway, back to Green theology. The crux of the matter, so my learned friends tell me, is the emphasis that has been placed on redemption rather than creation. Redemption, although pluralist in intent, is however singular in experience and the theory of creational theology is pluralist in outlook and pluralist in experience.

Roughly translated from scholasphere, I think what's being said is that the doctrine of the creation, through the Holy Spirit, includes in it a creation that's divine and therefore encourages partnership, not authorized rape. Which, when you apply to Disraeli's famous statement, 'if the choice is an ape or an angel, I am on the side of the angels,' means he may well have considered himself an angel but he was in fact behaving like an ape.

This argument is obviously very painful for the church which, since the Reformation, has been doing a sterling job in saving souls for Christ but quite clearly has appeared unconcerned that God's created world was being ripped to shreds by all those gentle saved Christian souls in the process. This is obviously a long, detailed discussion that needs to be had elsewhere.

Back onto firmer ground, the return of the counselling course, tonight was billed as 'healing through memories'. It's easy to forget among the deadlines and mental warfare that central to our being here is the power of Christ; we were reminded tonight what an awesome power that is and that none of us would survive half a minute in ministry without it. As our lacklustre grasp of the Holy Spirit was paraded before us we were numbed into silence, gagged by our pitiful faith. Healing through memories is a process where Christ is invited to intercede to heal within a counselling situation. The case histories presented to us were awesome. Christianity has survived because it works. The words of Christ have survived because they make a difference: 'Ask and the door will be opened'; 'When two or three are gathered together in my name I will be there with you'. As Christians we hear these statements all the time; they need polishing once in a while. We need reminding they are not just words, they are promises and when acted upon in faith we are given the key to this supreme healing love. I for one find those words in scripture probably the most terrifying of all.

The New Testament essay is done: 'Did Jesus expect an imminent end of the world?' I have this perverse habit of either choosing essay titles I fundamentally disagree with or the ones that theologically scare the living daylights out of me. Who would want to be a paid theologian, everyone picking your every word to pieces, attacking your ludicrous theories lovingly hewn from painful prayer? I wish I'd met one Professor Caird though, what a mind, a brave mind.

I spent the weekend with Poacher and an American exchange student called Daniel walking in the glories of Snowdonia. We'd planned the whole thing very badly—what we had overlooked was that it was the same weekend as 'The Three Peaks', an all-hours, all-weather, almighty yomp up in the mightiest mountains of the British Isles. We spent all the second night being woken up every fifteen minutes by hardened fell runners who seemed to choose our tent to stand next to and issue intricate instructions as to where they had left the batteries for their torch.

The last session of theology and practice of ministry was on church music. We are fortunate to be endowed with a man who without so much as a blink of an eye can rattle off ten different versions of 'Amazing Grace' without drawing breath. I still don't really understand why most contemporary church music seems to have been inspired by the theme tune to 'Emmerdale'. Worse still are the Christian bands; they may look hard on the outside, but there's always the suspicion that they're wearing crushed velvet underpants. The mass appeal of rock and roll is the suicidal lifestyle, sex and drugs and more drugs. Take away the pallid complexion of someone who has not seen a raw vegetable for twenty years and would not know what communion wine was if you threw it at him and you're really simply left with a bunch of good boys pretending to be tough 'n' hard. If *Songs of Fellowship and Praise* is where they are getting their lyrical inspiration from—and may I single out such gems here as 'Lord you put a tongue in my mouth'—then it's not surprising none of them have hit the big time. Contemporary Christian music need not imitate pop culture; it cannot succeed on that front; its roots do not feed off the numbing cocktail intravenously dripped into society by the music industry selling little girls' love and a frenzy of fashion. Christian music doesn't sweat; it appeals to your heart, not to your groin. We seem to have forgotten that hearts pump as well as feel and that the Holy Spirit dances with the dervishes.

All but two of the leavers have now got curacies. Leavers are those whose time is up and who will shortly be thrown into the real world of moving house again, meeting the congregation and paying the milk bill. There is a sense of sadness that really our time here is governed outwardly at least by our thinking and not by our feeling. For a bunch of people who are meant to be at ease with the love of God, we are at times icy cold. There are just thirteen days left before the final essay deadline; there are no excuses either.

Well, that's it. I put the pen down at one thirty last night. The essays are done. They have been stimulating, challenging and I must admit illuminating; I've definitely overcooked it a tad on 'The Church of England: Grey or Green?' however, it's done now, so that's that. All the essays are due in on Monday at twelve o'clock. The rest of the term is taken up with short courses with such illuminating titles as

'Older People and the Church' and 'The Deacon's Return' and the one I'm particularly looking forward to is 'The Devil Stole the Beat' (was he on drugs at the time?).

Last Wednesday we played the diocesan cricket team. Why is every vicar a cliché of a vicar? Knock-kneed, inoffensive and flat-footed. The young ones start off all right and then start this process of vicarization. Anyway it was a draw; they scored about eight runs off the last twenty overs.

Those people doing lofty degrees have disappeared into the shadows, they emerge at lunch looking like startled versions of the Milky Bar kid. Their workload is immense; essentially they have to complete an essay a week as well as doing all the other things a theological college demands.

After a last-minute panic which had me head-down in the wheelie bin desperately searching for the references which I was sure I had left on my desk, the essays were handed in. The reward for two and a half months hard labour was a day's fishing with Poacher. We caught nothing except the sun and a few backward glances of the spilled-milk-coated cows.

I miss Chapel; although it is enforced time with God it is nevertheless essential for maintaining this mysterious relationship. With my wife working I am really left picking up the scraps on Sundays. Praying must look very odd from the outside, what are we doing, what are we saying, eyes shut, hands clasped together? It's an act at best of being with God, of concentrating energy to be in his presence and at peace with that presence. It's communication without words, words are not necessary. God heals and speaks to us in feelings that emerge from the very centre of who we are. It is a different language and it does need to be learned. There are instances of course when God does speak directly to individuals in words. He has never spoken to me like that, but I have sensed his presence very deeply in the spaces that inhabit all of us.

When people speak of spiritual growth it is dependence on God they are really talking about. Although it may seem wrong and it may hurt, it is allowing God to be the first point of reference in your life. This can shatter everything you in fact believe in including God. God teaches love, breathes love. When Christians speak of this world being founded on love they are saying we live our life breathing the grace of God, there would be no life without that love, spiritual or physical—nothing.

Everyone doubts and the greater your faith the greater your doubts. It is easy to cite instances where the absence of God seems all too obvious, but we are not forced to believe, we cannot live life unless we are free, and free not to believe. We are free to do exactly as we please, whatever we want. 'God loves you' is not an easy answer to pain and suffering, it is at best a challenge to you as an individual to explore the possibilities of there being more to your life than the dictates of a free market and the Western obsession with pleasure. We are made much stronger through pain perhaps, more complete. There are painful decisions to make being a Christian, the ethics of materialism, the politics of sex and many others need addressing. What would our lives be like without Christianity? This society can go bashing on about how irrelevant it all seems, but let's not delude ourselves, it is still at the heart of almost everything we do and think.

The folly of having my vanity caressed with the old 'you are the only man for the job' routine came home to roost with the clash of the proposed Italian evening with a proposed Israeli dance class; the love child of these two protagonists was an evening in the common room eating bagel bacon sandwiches, listening to a CD of Israeli Eurovision song contest entries, drinking cheap Italian wine; sounds like an implausible plot for an indigestion tablet commercial.

The second problem was to persuade the house manager that a sports day in the college would be a good idea. He didn't look too enamoured initially, it wasn't until he realized the possibility of a Punch and Judy show for the children that his eyes lit up. I didn't tell him about the bicycle jousting; I thought I'd save that for a planning meeting.

Today is Ascension Day. The idea of Christ being raised bodily into the clouds I've always found intriguing. Consequently morning prayers were conducted from the organ gallery. There had been talk of winching the speaker up to the organ gallery whilst he was in midflow but that had been discarded.

It's a funny time really, half the college have finished their exams, whilst the other half are still locked up in the half-light swallowing books. It seems that without lectures the rhythm has gone and having studied so heavily for the last two and a half months you're suddenly catapulted into a vacuum.

We were hammered in the cricket: we made a grand total of 157 for 4 declared, their ex-Somerset batsmen clocked a cool 100 in ten overs; it was awesome. Beaten by the Baptists; it was a drubbing of immense proportions. The real needle match is this Saturday against another notoriously Evangelical theological college.

Well we won, drubbed them; it was all over by tea time, in fact they had the audacity to suggest we take our bowlers off to let them bat more easily; our captain declined.

Yesterday I was chatting to an elderly vicar who was taking a month's sabbatical. In theory the clergy are allowed a one-month sabbatical for every seven years worked. He was complaining about the hours many vicars are having to work and the strain this was putting on their families as well as their sanity.

It is indeed uncivilized and unrealistic to expect clergy to work the ludicrous hours that many of them do. A worn-out person is of no use to themselves or anybody else. Demands on your time are different if you have no responsibilities other than yourself, but if you are married with a family and have dependent relatives those relationships need quality time, love and care. Quite clearly the multi-parish system provides everyone with the worst of both worlds.

I have seen the results of over-work in my previous existence; people end up broken and scarred doing what they perceive as necessary to survive at the expense of themselves; we all do it, but if as a body we are opposed to Sunday trading for what I believe are the right reasons, then as a Christian body we must surely stop this rampant machoism that states unless you half kill yourself you're not doing your job properly.

If we are as Anglican churches allowing clergy to marry, then it must be accepted that those who are married will need to spend more time than the odd moment here and there with their partners if the marriage is to reflect the Christian values that it is under pressure to demonstrate.

There are still several people who have not found curacies. This is not good because there are no more vacancies. It means that some people will have to go on the dole and wait for a job to arrive. Frankly it's a mess. Having studied for two or three years, having gone through a rigorous and in many cases traumatic selection process, having given up jobs, families and friends, the Church I feel should be a lot more organized on this front. It is not as if we have too many vicars; we have too few.

Now that lectures are over we're all being cajoled into various short courses. I've just had two days of ageing. Old people are not what the media present them as. No surprises on that front. Of course our lack of consideration is woeful, but what seems to be emerging as well is that our imagination and our creativity also run the risk of being rendered incompetent by our preconceptions.

We were asked to describe our feelings when we first arrived at theological college. These ranged from confusion, depression, freedom, through to a feeling of being disturbed, alienated and isolated (no surprise on that front either).

The lecturer then dropped the bombshell that these emotions were for the most part identical to those of people who had neared the end of their working lives and were retiring. Then we all were led open-mouthed through the politics which boiled down to money set aside for the care for the elderly to come. Forget it: there isn't going to be any; it's cheaper to visit people than to look after them. Old people will be, simply because of the ageing population, a greater part of any future ministry and yet 80 per cent of all evangelism is aimed at the young, especially those who it's felt will have pivotal roles in the shaping of future society.

Saturday was open day for all those coming to this theological college next year. It was my job as social secretary to offer enlightening information on the year's packed and rumbustious social calendar.

It's difficult to explain to any fair degree what theological college is like in fifteen minutes. It's like an astronaut trying to make you feel like you're walking on the moon. I don't envy them starting, it is a lonely experience. I've never been to university but I would imagine it's very different with discos and student beer. The church doesn't really go in for that. I'm still fighting to discover if there is a pleasure principle that extends beyond reading and gardening. Seeing them was rather like going to a wedding as a married couple. The thrill is the naive, beautiful, hopeful love that's there tearing the back of your throat out for all to see. It bears no relevance to marriage and even less, I would think, to virginity.

Seeing the assembled faces of next year's intake is the same. Yes God is still at work calling all those who look like vicars anyway and some that don't, but it's still happening; it proves you're not mad and that this beautiful gritty and threatening love is still pointing at people and dragging them kicking and crying to the altar. You can't tell them that the academic work will suck out their insides and then hang them out to dry, or that they will doubt; that what they hold dear will be kicked to pieces in front of them.

I bawled at the prayer lady on Friday afternoon. She was brilliant, pointing her finger and squeezing the establishment into insignificant droplets. There are so many words here, you get swamped by them. I was drowning in them. They are words, only words, that's all. I'd forgotten that. God was being distilled to theory, reduced to history, Jesus no more than a polished schizophrenic, a revolutionary socialist, the resurrection was dreamed, the miracles are metaphors, the Pentecost poetic. I'd hit the wall. I was doing maths with all its dry numbers. My faith was being squeezed into boxes of convenience easily packed off to some poor unsuspecting parish. She took a sledgehammer to all of them. These notions were man-made, every one. They'll try to slip back into their canary cages safe from approaching claws, but it's a brighter bird that's free. What a week. Monday exploded with a three-hour lecture on Islam and 'its worldwide millions'; Tuesday was a sustained and quite brutal attack on the ethics of advertising and the great first/third world divide; Wednesday was the immense and turbulent bravery of Christians under communism—what a dark shadow that has cast over the world. Yesterday was the 'It's a Knockout combined with the children's party' and today we have the end of term service, dinner and review.

Those of us remaining were taken through the shape of

our last year this morning: we can forget summer. I have a one-month parish attachment. Three essays, one report and an all-week ecumenical introduction session. My wife is also having a baby right in the middle of all of that.

The 'It's a Knockout' seemed a great success, Poacher hit the Pimms pretty hard and the bicycle jousting went particularly well. It had cost me a serious session in the Hat and Feathers with the house manager. I don't think either of us remember the small print which under the circumstances was just as well. Mad Dog, who was the E team's chosen jouster, looked particularly fetching on the back seat of a tandem in his well-worn bicycle helmet clutching a dustbin lid. We thought we'd ticked all the boxes on the safety front, head shots and tampering with your opponent's tandem were not allowed. But in the final joust Mad Dog nearly garrotted his opponent when his lance, which was a broom with a pillow wrapped round the end of it, snapped on impact. It was a good afternoon; we had a break in the weather and the proverbial tea on the lawn. I know it sounds like a fête; more worrying was that it did begin to resemble one—all we needed was a creaky PA system and a jam stall and no one would have known the difference.

Don't think would-be vicars are not prone to bending the rules and cheating in the egg and spoon race. They are. Don't think they're all terribly helpful and volunteer to help clear up afterwards. They're not. By and large, it's the same people who do everything. Not a great advertisement, dare I say the word, for the body of Christ but concrete proof we are horribly human. Next year I have the heady delights of the resurrection, a visit to the undertakers, ethics, doctrine and worship to look forward to. I have to say I couldn't even grasp the first two lines explaining the doctrine timetable, let alone what the rest of it meant.

June 1993

I passed all the essays. I was disappointed they weren't really the honourable passes I was hoping for. I did work hard and the essays only really served to highlight how much I don't know and my lamentable lack of being able to write an essay and spell Deuteronomy. I've come to the conclusion that writing essays is rather like passing a driving test. There is obviously a technique to essay writing and I don't have it. I'm sure it can be acquired nonetheless. The question is: do I spend my final year of two learning it or is muddling through, academically at least, all that's needed?

I'm not convinced that the church really benefits pastorally from all these frightfully logical people with the bedside manner of an abacus. In fact (here comes the academic argument) it would appear the church has been declining since the rigorous training given by the Theological Colleges was introduced. So they don't appear to have really been a great success as yet. My true gripe is that I'm not convinced that an academic theological approach to ministry has anything startling to offer above a spiritual, prayerful and pastoral approach. The academic upper hand of the moment is demonstrated by every theological college timetable in the country and what we appear to have ended up with as a result is undoubtedly an immensely learned church hierarchy who quite clearly are capable of supporting ontological arguments and other such unpronounceable academic positions, but these have little to do with an assembly line or a bar in Covent Garden.

The return of the priests and the deacons was interesting. They were all ex-students and their brief was to tell it like it is wrapped up behind a dog collar. I bunked the session last night, it was the polite one with the staff. The truth usually takes time. This morning I flitted from one group to another, listening to where the lines were drawn. Most of them were still on honeymoon, they all said the doorbell went a lot and the phone rang and they all intimated that theological college had nothing in common with ministry. I spent most of the time watching their partners. They are the ones who are left alone in a strange house as their other halves are out for the fourth evening in a row. You could see it in their eyes, you could sense the isolation that comes with having to be polite all the time.

Well they've all gone, just under half the college have left. There has been a succession of vans leaving all day stuffed full of books, B & Q lampshades and assorted worn chairs. Some are going to London, one or two are off to Wales, Mad Dog's gone to a collection of parishes in Wiltshire and the others are scattered all over the place. There are three of them without jobs who will have to wait and see if anything comes up in the autumn, it's not that likely. We had a very emotional farewell communion, a meal and the review where the Principal won the 'best dressed member of college' award. The rest of us have one more week left and then it's parish attachments.

We haven't had our traditional quiet day this term. During one such quiet day I was told an ordinand waltzed into a very quiet dining room wearing a Walkman. He was immediately confronted by a member of staff who reprimanded him for listening to music, saying it wasn't really in the spirit of the day. He casually took off his headphones and placed them over the ears of his accuser. The Walkman was playing a blank tape. Marvellous.

My academic interview damp-squibbed. I'm to be given lessons on how to construct a dry, logical, squeaky-clean argument. It's my own fault; it's what comes from leaving school at sixteen.

I've volunteered to make a video which is to go towards my collection of points to gain my certificate. The magic number is twenty-six. They're awarded on every subject. I think I might have half by now.

I remember being told at the start of the year that a month off in the summer is essential. This, frankly, does not look like it's going to materialize.

The publicity committee was as humourless as ever. There were eight of us this time, reluctantly arranged in the Celtic Christianity room. Our task was the text of the brochure. It was suggested at the beginning of the meeting that group analysis of the copy was not the best way forward and after about forty-five minutes of contradicting each other, the chairman, to everyone's supreme relief, elected himself editor. We then repeated the first conversation we'd had six weeks earlier on the logo. I then suggested we needed a budget, this I think was agreed and as we kept on being reminded how potentially important this was, I also recommended some designers. To be honest, all does not bode well. I had the distinct impression I was being tolerated and that my previous experience was not altogether welcome, and whatever suggestions might have been entertained at the time the end result would ultimately be commissioned on the grapevine for the cost of a raisin and bear a passing resemblance to a lemon. We'll wait and see.

It's over, the year is done, there's one more to go. On Tuesday I start what's called an attachment where I fall dutifully behind a real vicar and find out what life is really like in a dog collar.

It has been the best year of my life, no regrets. I know Norman Lamont said that and came a cropper, but I'm never likely to be the Chancellor of the Exchequer.

I'm still deeply suspicious of the labels that divide us: Evangelical, Anglo-Catholic and the others. I accept that they form a spiritual basis for some but from what I have seen so far, most people end up hooked on the dogma of their own adopted tradition. But far more dangerous is the fact that the church uses up most of its energy servicing its divisions and disagreements, courting compromise at the expense of everything else, and it is this sapping unproductive politics that has so decimated our purpose and our imaginations. The only firm decision I've come to is a profound loathing of the Book of Common Prayer. It's a meaningless charade and we should have the courage to put it on the top shelf. It is the language of yesterday and simply serves to reinforce all those dreadful clichés about lisping vicars. Apart from my firm BCP decision I am totally undecided about everything else. I do find myself going over my calling, dissecting the strands, the course of events, just to make sure it really did happen and it wasn't some wild dream.

However there is also a growing sense of crisis. It's easy to want to give things up. I can almost remember standing on the outside before theological college basking in the poetic vision and the shock on people's faces. The reality is of course far more brutal. Our drastically reduced income and separation from friends have left bruises we are beginning to feel. I cannot nip out in a fit of romantic pique and buy my wife a present. I could but we wouldn't eat. Wallowing in sexual hedonism even for a second has its own penalties. Looking up at the top shelf of the newsagents is out of bounds: temptations are much harder to deal with simply because there's no excuse for not dealing with them. It's not something you can simply have a holiday from; there is no release; the spiritual pressure is immense. It's not a job, it's a way of life. You cannot do the job without living the Christian life. It's twenty-four hours a day, 365 days a year for as long as I live and breathe. You are caught in the shadows of society, neither in it nor out of it, once you have broken free from fashion, politics, street credibility, ambitions and all the other insignificant dictates of our free society. It's not easy. You see, they are comfortable things, you know where you are with them. You simply have to obey all the rules and play the game. Without them, however, you're floating free; having never done it before it is not altogether a pleasant experience; letting go of those ropes is surprisingly difficult. However, let them go you must, they're just holding you down and, as was said in the first sermon of the year—he stood there shaking his fist at us—you will have to give up a part of you. Yes, you do, he was absolutely right; a part of you does go. It is painful, even harder if you fight it; it's a battle you cannot win.

But by far the most pressing problem I face at the moment is rapidly failing confidence in the way the church presents itself. The church is constantly trying to impress upon me and everybody else that Christ through his Holy Spirit is alive now, a face of grace and beauty that's present at the very moment you are reading this. I am reconciled to that. I believe the grace of God is with us always. I am not reconciled to the fact that for its direction and inspiration the church spends the majority of its time looking back over its shoulder, donning scholastic glasses to see through the mists of time in its attempt to justify its actions as truly Christian. The naive belief that the early church held in some sense the holy Christian grail is ludicrous. If we are dealing with a living God we must stop acting as if he died 2000 years ago. The rationale that suggests he can be conjured up out of antiquity via the language of the sixteenth century is folklore, not faith. I am convinced that a gracious God responds to the efforts of his children whatever the language. I'm just not altogether sure whether in our passion for the past we may not perhaps have forgotten the present.

If God is with us he is with us in the present, concerned

for the present. Each living moment belongs to God, is God. The arrogant belief that we can discern his character through dissecting his actions is dangerous. Can a child know the mind of his father? Perhaps that is what makes Christ so beautiful. Quite clearly his relationship with God was complete. He was killed by tradition, not shackled to it.

September 1993

Here we are again or rather here we go again. Some summer. There are now four of us. Jonson arrived at seven o'clock in the morning on 19 August. Everything else seems a distant memory apart from the staircase meeting this morning.

I spent the regulation month in a parish; the vicar was a wonderful man. It was everything I hoped it would be, a shambles, enlightening, difficult, embarrassing and above all humbling. Like most Christian principles it all happened in reverse. I arrived armed with a year at theological college ready to do everything and I left a month later realizing just how incapable I am at doing anything. Above all I found the whole experience immensely humbling.

The new lot all seem very sensible, there's one chap with a flowery shirt, beads and torn jeans, and there's a very freaky lady guitarist who wears a lot of tight black. But the rest of them look like the sort of people you see in Texas Homecare on a Sunday afternoon.

Spiritually it's been a rollercoaster summer. It's not so much the heeby-jeebies about there being no escape—I can down tools right now—it's the price that's frightening. I'm sure all of us have second thoughts, third thoughts and monstrous doubts. But there is no way out: suffering seems to be an inextricable part of the Christian equation. It's how you deal with that pain that ultimately spears you or spares you. This is the sharp end, the buck stops here. We are servants of God and humanity and all we have to offer ultimately to both is ourselves.

I've changed studies and studymates: Poacher and I are entombed in billowing smoke in a room that manages some afternoon sun. It's not a radical step; however, it will change the nature of Friday morning prayers. The member of staff attached to our new group is no less than the Principal. He complained to me this morning he woke up with an 'Attilla the Hun' sticker stuck to the back of his Isle of Sheppey jumper. I think he was implying that at last night's introductory Bar-b-que 'guess who you are' competition that it had been an intentional move on my part as social secretary to issue him with Attilla the Hun. I naturally told him that these things came out at random. Yes, while I was writing the tickets out it was one of those random thoughts that just came to me.

October 1993

Christianity brandishes a double-edged sword, there is nowhere to run except God, so in that respect it's hardly surprising that Christians speak of giving their pain to God, which is only fair since the moral dilemma is in most cases precipitated by faith and any serious relationship with Christ's Holy Spirit. Christian communities and Christian consciousness are in most instances the opposite to what they would appear. At best we do not concentrate on the judgment of others—that is not our business; we are neutral, we have to be. We do not chastise the drug addict, the alcoholic, the murderer, the thief and however unpleasant the rapist may be we must and do pray for them, love them. Then the legacy of the love of Christ is that by love we are being healed and fashioned and as Christians we implore that same love to weave its healing presence even in the darkest places. If it is unable to pierce the darkest corners in all of us then the journey of our faith, faith itself, is worthless, built on sand.

Once it has you in its clutches, as C.S. Lewis would say, there can be no return. Once the light even the smallest spark has revealed our potential for the most dreadful things imaginable we can see them for what they are. We are forced to face them. In some people this takes a second and others it takes years. I do believe God works in each one of us and as long as there is this healing, this reconciling of our lives to that body, to that source, that love, then there is always hope; hope can never be vanquished.

Today we spent time at each other's colleges loosely dancing around the topic as to why some of us are Methodists, United Reformed, Charismatic, Evangelical, Anglo-Catholics and, no wonder, confused. It was an illuminating discussion. The nuts and bolts of it were that perhaps we have all been called to a particular ministry. That is to say that if the group dynamic was to stand on your head and spin then God perhaps would call people with strong necks and a wonderful sense of balance to minister within this style. If there are groups of people centred around particular styles of worship, it should perhaps not be surprising that certain individuals are called to minister in that style. I think the problem arises when one group quite naturally perceives the other groups as a few jelly babies short of the full packet. I feel God is happy to receive us as we are, raw, crying, speaking in tongues to Deep Purple, Evangelical, Anglo-Catholic, whatever, as long as we mean it; as long as our hearts are earnestly seeking a dialogue, this language is going to be in a thousand tongues.

The football season is upon us once again. As part of 'mission' five of us crammed into a four-person car and spent all evening playing indoor four-a-side football at a Christian-run youth club.

I woke up this morning feeling that I'd been mauled by a medicine ball. But we held our own, won 3 lost 2. It was a great place. The bloke running it had a good attitude. He sort of took the line that psychotic acts of violence on the indoor football arena were the norm for this environment. So any appeal to his refereeing sensibilities having been taken out against the wall by two six-foot-four skinheads was not likely to get a sympathetic hearing.

The Chinese evening meal at the Principal's was a roaring success. This was primarily for all the new ordinands. I remember going last year, dewy-eyed and nervous. The Principal had asked someone else to speak on life at theological college when you're married with children. He came down with flu so I was dropped in at the last moment. I basically had four points. The first one was that everything that says it's compulsory isn't. At this juncture the Principal said in a loud voice, 'Now you know why we originally asked Anthony Spencer to come' and then put his head in his hands.

I haven't had a lecture yet and my mind feels like overcooked rhubarb. The meeting with the director of studies did not go well. He didn't so much shoot my idea of a video down, he more dismembered it in front of me. His tactics were those of a prairie dog. He wore me down with doctrine, confused my senses with ethics, frightened me with final year ministry, saving the *coup de grâce* of double psychology to finish me off. This year's lectures look utterly terrifying.

I have a doctrine essay on the incarnation to complete by next Wednesday. Looking at the current debate between the divinity and humanity of Christ, was he human, was he divine or, as it states in the creed, was he both? And what is lost if we lose this 1,500-year-old agreement that Christ is both human and divine?

My strategy for the term is to front-load everything. So I have this blitz at presiding over staircase prayers, leading Chapel, cooking common-room supper, washing up common-room tea, serving at one of the dinners and the rest of it all within the first three weeks. That should hopefully give me the rest of the term to get my brain around what I'm actually being asked to consider in the lectures. I have a feeling it's all going to go horribly wrong and what with the nocturnal activities of a seven-week-old human being, fireworks night, football and, most importantly, my wonderful wife, one of the previous list is going to backfire terribly.

College communion this evening was more surreal than usual: we started with some Irish folk music; it then became apparent that the guest violinist was struggling to hit the right notes. The generously proportioned bald headed man on my left who was wearing bright green tracksuit bottoms and a white T-shirt didn't sing a note for the first two hymns so I was completely unprepared for his operatic harmonies at full volume in the third. His tracksuit bottoms were not designed for the high notes and in any other capacity he would have been arrested for indecent exposure. In trying to contain my mirth I turned to the right where another bald headed man clearly didn't see the funny side of my predicament.

The doctrine essay is done. It nearly took me over the edge. To be honest I've been standing there looking into the rough seas wondering whether to jump or not. This has probably been the most difficult time I've had. I know I have to go through it, it's the marathon runner's wall and in part the syllabus here is designed to make you face it, that's fair enough; if you can't survive here in a Christian community closeted by concern, cotton-wooled by routine, pampered with religion then I would imagine the periods of stabbing doubt away from this bed of nails will rupture your heart.

The doctrine essay raised some serious questions, a Jewish writer in fact opened the door. He noted that it was all very well for Christ to preach 'love your enemy' and, undoubtedly coming out in a blaze of empathy, drew my attention to the fact that there is not one place where Christ practises what he preaches contained within the New Testament. Now that may be a standard criticism and Christ's obvious love for the lost is well documented. But clearly he's not over-enamoured with the Jews who were running the temple in Jerusalem at the time.

This led me on to a second question. It's all very well to say no fornication (sex out of wedlock) but I feel I need an explanation as to why the ten commandments, on examination, appear to read as a decree from a dictator. There is no explanation given. Clearly, at the time they were issued, any violation of the commandments resulted in instant death. I wrote an essay last year on 'How could the God of love kill?' based around the exploits of one Joshua who, three and a half thousand years ago, had no qualms about going into a community and massacring every living thing, men, women, children and animals under the ferocious flag of the Jewish 'Ban'. The doctrine essay also raised the question of hell. Can a God of love condemn? I believe in Christianity in part because I feel that there is forgiveness, not at a price, that price has been paid by Christ; that the murderer and the saint are received mercifully and that the saint needs that mercy just as much as the murderer. That the sins of the saint taken in the context of belief are just as great. That doesn't mean to say that I in any way condone murder. I don't feel it's right to condemn people because of our failure and, make no mistake, it is our failure. If we are charged with believing and spreading the word of Christ's love for this world then a simple head count on Sunday mornings would suggest we are failing to deliver. Again I don't see a problem with the content, the message of Christ, it is the mode of delivery in the context of the society we are living in that is quite obviously not working. We also, I feel, have to be a little more generous to those who practise other faiths than regarding them as headless chickens destined for hell. Fundamentalisms on both sides of the divide can only accelerate this creeping animosity. Christianity's claim to own our God at the expense of everything else needs to be examined; it may well be that the threat posed by a multi-faith society to an, at best, static Christian population will force us to abandon our petty Christian differences and face the real issues of a world desperately seeking some sense from the appalling domination of business interests. There are no answers to these questions, only opinions. There is nothing concrete to get hold of and throw at people when they hit you with them; when you have to cremate someone who felt the whole shooting match was designed to make the frightened comfortable. At the end of the day you are left with your faith despite the obvious contradictions to it and St Peter's threats of consuming your own vomit if you abandon it. Why do we say it's easy? We sell it as easy, believe in me and you will have eternal life sounds so simple, painless. It's just a ticket; if you buy it, you have a long journey ahead of you over some very rough ground indeed. I have this dreadful feeling we've made it pretty, all smiles and flowers. We forget that Christianity is riddled with agony.

Bart is looking very grey around the gills. He's doing a three-year course and was telling me that he plans to spend next term working at a mental hospital. He is sharing a study with someone who is having a lot of problems reconciling who they were, what they were and what they are to become. It is getting very bloody.

I went to London last night and attended the British media environmental awards. They were very good. The Secretary of State, John Gummer, mounted the podium having publicly abandoned his prepared speech and verbally set off in the direction of the unscripted. For a moment there I detected a man of sincerity through what he was saying. He stumbled over the notion of a car-crazy economy. The reality is of course he has both hands tied behind his back by the system he has inherited. The system that swamps us all, the system that by crying individuality at the altar of the media has in fact rendered us no more than slaves to consumerism. All the magazines that tell us what is fashion, fun, an acceptable orgasm, the newspapers that dictate what is right; we've all become crazy in allowing them to think for us. The freedom they tout is on their terms. They have locked us into a room with pictures of themselves on the walls; they feed us agony and sensation to convince us we can feel. This diet is making us paranoid; they are teaching us to fear, that's all. They tell us it's fun. 'Just a bit of fun,' they say. We've believed them for far too long.

I left at about half past one. Looking into the eyes of the night, I hadn't seen stars like those for years—there in the naked universe, struggling with sense, setting fire to the silences. They will not be numbed by time. I always wonder what they look like in America.

I travelled with an old friend down to London. His name is Thomas Merton. He's dead now. His autobiography was the first so-called Christian book I ever read. It influenced me deeply. He sweats God.

He was a Cisterian monk with immense vision and staggering humanity. But above all I think he was a writer. Not the bone-dry academic variety that reduces Christ to the logical and our response to the plausible. I admit it needs to be done, that we have to wrestle with these questions in a dry, logical manner. Thomas Merton, however, talks to my heart, not to my mind. He is saved by his continual willingness to be drawn into the simplicity and awe of God's love. He manages to purvey a sense of God in everything. His idea that the judgment of God is ongoing rather than pronounced from on high is very interesting. We see the creation as having happened at a certain time, we have structured periods, Jurassic and so on. We talk about evolution as if we are the zenith, that it ends with humanity. We are in fact part of a continuum. God's creation surely happens every second, it is now, we are living in it as it happens. That is very different to it having happened in Genesis chapter one. If we leave it at Genesis chapter one that is where we leave God as far as creation is concerned. There are understandable qualms about worshipping creation as God. But as it says in *Lux Mundi*, either God is everywhere present in nature or he is nowhere. He cannot be here and not here.

Why have we sectioned off religious writing into religious bookshops? It is almost as if God has no place among D.H. Lawrence and Jackie Collins. What a terrible mistake that has been. We've done it to art as well. Christian art it's called, music too. There are Christian bands hived off from the rest of the music industry, it's religious prejudice. We wear our religion on our sleeve; we slap it all over the canvas; it pours from our pen; we're a different type of creative personality. What a load of tosh, was not God in the agony of Van Gogh, in the hands of Jimi Hendrix, in the pen of Bruce Chatwin and the ragged stance of Johnny Rotten?

Lonely? Christian? Join a lonely Christian singles club. Now that sounds like a bundle of laughs if ever there was one. No sex, a glass of cider and an evening in with the best of Billy Graham. Why can't Christians join the usual dating agencies? You know, get out there, mix it up a bit with all the rest of the world.

The moment Christianity becomes a club, by its very nature it excludes those who are not in it. I was under the impression the message of Christ was for everyone.

The curacy crisis has hit. I've had to turn down two potential jobs on the strength of a telephone call. The parish vicar in the first job described himself as a 'conservative bigot'. I only wish he had been joking; he wasn't. The second vicar took exception to my wife not being a practising Christian; not a lot of common ground there either. Poacher has just spent a weekend in Shropshire with a potential employer who by all accounts sounded natural, perceptive and understanding. Maybe I've just had a bad run.

Another curacy popped through the post this morning complete with an accompanying letter from my DDO telling me not to turn down jobs on the phone. I have tried to explain on several occasions that pairing me with 'conservative bigots' and squeezing me into the 'paranoid of pagans' brigade will simply not work. Anyway third time lucky. Otherwise it's the vagaries of the open market for me. I've had a look at all the jobs that have arrived at college so far. It's no surprise they all happen to be either so Anglo-Catholic the envelopes were just about incense-scented or so extremely Evangelical that every sentence had a biblical reference dripping off the end of it. Most of us in training are not that extreme; it's not surprising therefore that the diocese has been unable to fill these vacancies from within. This is the usual crop of curacies that end up at theological colleges and by and large they are not a pretty sight.

I was privileged to sit next to someone in our weekly college communion who was praying in Tongues. Tongues is described by the apostle Paul as a spiritual gift. It is a visual and verbal manifestation of the Holy Spirit working in you whilst you pray. He sat with his mouth twitching, his lips whispering, his body occasionally jolting. It appeared more of a giving of your whole self to God in prayer; it didn't seem to be that God had taken over, it appeared a completely natural reaction to an overwhelming recognition of the presence of the Holy Spirit. Prayer is learning the language of God, it is not something that is individual; by that I mean it is the communication of our human being with the being of God and it is in itself a state of being. The Holy Spirit in my experience is physical. There is a definite sense of someone else praying with you. This presence is able to touch the essence of who you are and what you are in the eyes of God; the hope of God in you, the hope of God for you is made possible through prayer.

I'm afraid I dropped my bucket with one of the lecturers on the worship course. Eight of us have been asked to recreate a third-century baptism based on Saint Ambrose. I went to apologize this morning and was told politely but firmly that I would not be able to do that sort of thing in a parish. I stuck to my guns and insisted politely but firmly that to ask eight people, none of whom had the first idea how to write a script let alone act convincingly, was unrealistic, especially as the whole project has to be ready in ten days time. I was then privy to an illuminating talk on church politics and how if I kept my head down and 'played the game' I could usurp the system, but it was essential I weave my way into the whispering rather than throw myself at it. The trouble, as I was told in no uncertain terms, is the absence of a salary, a decent financial reward. The importance of position and one's supposed authority becomes all the more critical in demonstrating sadly to the clerical beings concerned that what they say and who they are is justified by the job they do. Yet the church clearly does seem to be ill with people dancing around between working parties spouting importance.

The Arch-Evangelical and I crossed swords over the issue of mission. It was a confrontation conducted by the ballet school of duelling. He felt that mission was the only justifiable occupation for Christian ministers. I hit him with a hermit and then struck him again with an entire enclosed order of monks. Saying that surely they had been called by God. His eyebrows scoffed a little but he didn't listen and sadly neither did I.

What a week. It's Friday evening. The doctrine lectures are proving to be utterly mindblowing with cyclonic repercussions and say it I must, the lecturer concerned is nothing short of clear, concise, and, above all, inspiring. These lectures make a difference. I'm not convinced it's a science, it feels more like art. We looked at kingship, the majesty of the divine. We talk about King, Saviour, Redeemer. These words are loaded, primed by history and essentially meaningless today. I find myself singing on a very regular basis 'My God and King' 'Jesus is Lord', however it's not what I'm saying it's how I'm saying it. I'm trying to express something beyond words. T.S. Eliot said, quite rightly I feel, that words simply cannot take the weight of what we are trying to say, they cannot contain the meaning. They crack under the pressure. But our problems are greater than that. Western culture has a low view of royalty; this is a combination of our ravenous appetite for their inside leg measurements and who in fact has been doing the measuring, combined with the gross double standards of the national press who shout 'morality' whilst pushing the opium of scandal and the narcotics of naughty nights out, feeding the voyeur with one breath and asking for his castration with the next. In this orgy of insanity to align Jesus Christ liturgically with the standing of the royal family is asking for trouble. It boils down to worldviews. Christians have a Christian worldview and what we're trying to do is ask you to take a look at what we see. However, we're on to a loser here as far as 'king' is concerned; is heaven a republic? Is hell a dictatorship? Democracies such as ours place a high price on our fickle freedom. We tend to tout heaven as a dictatorship, supreme authority and all that.

However our view of authority is limited by all the demigods of our age. The authority of Christ is more subtle, perhaps weaker than that. That's why it's so beautiful.

The new ordinands are quite a lively bunch. One of them is fresh from the House of Commons. In his previous existence he was a researcher for an MP, he was the bloke at the open day who sat there cool as a caterpillar dripping with love beads. He had some friends up for the weekend who were obviously unfamiliar with the niceties of theological college. 'Suck my dick' was their parting gift spelled out in fridge magnets in the kitchen on the most conservative staircase in the college. Its author apparently worked for an MP, the question is what party? It could be any of them, I suppose.

I'm off to meet the vicar on Monday, he wants someone who's fizzing for Christ.

I've just read some of what went before; all of it, most of it stinks. It looked like the don't let them change you brigade were losing. I don't think they will. I smoke too much for that. What do you want dear reader; what do you want from me, a picture of God, the nails of Christ? what do you want to hear, that religion is sweet, suffering fashions grace? prayer is beautiful? Where are you in all of this?

The reality is we're left inventing order; it's our order, matins, compline, all of it drenched in compromise because of what we cannot be certain of; we convince each other to join this madness, yes, we can spur each other on with eloquence, insight, charity. But it's lonely; it's a lonely path, I know that, there are so many lonely eyes here. It can be made fun by football, amusing for you at the sight of the Principal's tank-tops. We've done a good job at making this unbearable love bearable, we've ordered it nicely for you, given it kind words. They are kind, the Holy Spirit is kind. But you will be left pulling the stars out of the sky on your own, no one can help you do that. It's something you have to bear. Life is full of agonies. I imagine they have a reason. Yes the light of Christ is beautiful but it will tear out the bits in you that are killing him, to prepare you far beyond your death.

I'm not convinced God is complicated; intricate maybe, but we are shielded from him by no more than ourselves locked in battle with our vanity, gasping as the flesh demands another hit of sex, food, more cigarettes and a beautiful view trapped by our birth on one side and our death on the other. There is little time to get used to the noise, little time to acquaint oneself with true peace. We carry the burden of consciousness around like a cocked pistol. Some of us wound other people, some of us wound ourselves, all of us in the West wound our neighbours in the Third World firing recklessly into the distance beyond, where we can't see the damage we're doing.

It's been a remarkably still autumn. There hasn't been any wind as such to nudge the leaves from the end of the branches. Even in the heart of the city the colours are haunting, throwing vivid yellows and deep reds at your senses chilling them with their sadness. The pain of my own wretchedness plagues my imagination continually with a way out, an escape from this viceless grip and the drip of understanding smiles. It is becoming an endurance test.

The saga of my outburst at having to write a play continues. It has since reached my ear that it has been taken as personal, so much so that I must be anti the ordination of women and other such manly causes.

To be honest I think there's a hidden agenda here, not mine; this is the whispering campaign which in fact does no more than to unmask its own paranoia; what a pity. I duly climbed the stairs and presented my case to the Principal of the theological college where the whispering echoes were loudest and made my case. He was immensely reasonable. I've always liked him. He was glad I came and that the air had been exorcised of this unhappy situation.

I spent the rest of the day doing penance and writing the play from some very good notes provided by some of the students who hadn't felt this was such a tall order. There's another doctrine essay to complete within the next two weeks and I'm reading Revelation chapter three tomorrow morning. There's fireworks on Thursday night but most importantly 'The Buddha of Suburbia' hits the television at 9.30 tomorrow night. Life in the Seventies. David Bowie has written the theme music, who could forget the make-up?

Well, the third possibility of a curacy has ended with a charming, short and cryptic letter. It was posted the day after I met the vicar, his wife and their two-year-old son. It was a lovely church. I thought he was a very fine man, his wife wore it well. But I felt also, this wasn't said, that once again it was my wife that was the stumbling block. The fact that she doesn't go to church seems to send all sorts of shivers down

Evangelical spines and very frail they must be too. I can see the logic of a committed husband and wife team wanting a committed husband and wife curate team. There are two problems here really: one, the church does not pay my wife, it pays me: voluntary work is voluntary and that also implies that it is not unreasonable if my wife volunteers not to do it. Point two, does God love my wife less because she happens not to come to church? Becoming a vicar is a vocation. Does a loving God tap you on the shoulder in isolation from the circumstances around you? I do not believe so.

I have heard many people say that they have been called as a partnership and that's brilliant. However, I also feel that because my faith naturally impacts upon the way that I love my wife, I have a justifiable claim on that partnership; it is impossible for me as I am to do the job without my wife. OK some people may say I have a responsibility to evangelize to her, to insist that Christ is Lord and her life is meaningless without that. She's not without that, she's married to an ordinand. However, much more important than any of my reasons are her reasons. The whole concept of a loving God collapses completely if, as human beings, we are not free to make our own choices about that God, and just because somebody does not believe in going to church every Sunday cannot detract from the love of God for them. By making that distinction ourselves, by separating the churched from the unchurched, and that is all it is, we are firstly loving God on our terms and secondly limiting the love of God to those people who go to church. Our expansive view of Christ as Lord of all creation and God the Father becomes limited by our definition of what that all means. The Pharisees surely made the same mistake, they became attached to models of worship, love became law, they reduced God to a mathematical equation.

The Principal is always going on about Christianity being reflected in people's lifestyles. I agree: I believe that it should be as well. But I believe any signs of Christian maturity should be as a result of personal decision: they should never be imposed by an outside force or regulated by one. Religious totalitarianism is a particularly ugly animal; we have seen it raise its cruel intolerance throughout history, usually ending up in self-justifying acts of violence and whole hosts of other equally distasteful actions in support of divine megalomania. We will never be able to convince anyone of a personal loving God if we behave in an impersonal authoritarian fashion. Worst of all the thick end of this wedge assumes that we all follow the same path to the cross of Christ. The Church of England would not be in existence if that were the case. Paul's pain was quite clearly different to Peter's. My wife will make her peace with God in her own time, in her own way and at her own pace; she's an adult human being. She has been given the freedom of humanity by God. She's entitled to exercise that freedom in any way she chooses. Take away that choice and you take away her dignity too. I can understand from a practical point of view that might not be easy for the ministerial husband and wife team to accept. But the true reality is they have excluded her from their church.

We had the delights of the publicity committee after lunch, it took about thirty seconds before the feeling of pushing treacle uphill submerged the flicker of dogged optimism. I asked vainly whether or not a budget had been approved for the design work but it all became painfully clear when the chairman suggested we trawl our friends for a favour what sort of brochure this was going to be; it was already a brochure that nobody wanted. Without a budget it means that no one is accountable and I have this dreadful foreboding that we will all be sentenced to another sunset or tortured by a stencilled tulip. The copy seems to be chugging along down the corridors of power without spilling too much red ink; that's the easy part really. Try this for size. 'Since we have already severed the link (in this life) between epistemological and sotieriological necessities, to argue the epistemological and revelational inadequacy of non-constructive views is hardly sufficient to meet the point at issue.'

Welcome to doctrine. Now you know why vicars look like they've been physiologically disturbed by a Scrabble board. Doctrine is about finding an intellectual pathway into the mind of God. It gets its directions from secret maps enshrined in Christian creeds where all words are unable to take the pressure of their implied meaning. Consequently new words, invariably bigger words, have been inserted to cut out the necessity for pages of smaller words. I can't help feeling if God wanted us to have the combination, if there is such a thing, he would have been a little more forthcoming with it in the first place. The crucial question is: has doctrine taken us any further along the road to God? or has it merely been going round in intellectual circles keeping pace with humanity's ideas about God? I tend to feel we have all we need here of God, so why complicate the issue? It's stimulating stuff and once you learn to pronounce words like sotieriological it will catapult your mind into previously uncharted dilemmas and your throat into long marathon nights of intense discussion.

You see questions like what was exactly taking place on the cross are so tantalizing because there is no answer. If Jesus' resurrection is really the icing on the cake, the Hollywood bit, the justification, what was being justified? The love of God? the sin of humanity? the redemption of creation? Are the effects of the crucifixion relevant to those who don't believe in it? And if so, how, and if how, why, and why did Christ not tell us, did God tell him not to? What does this say of God and how does that reflect on his relationship with Jesus and how did that reflect on Jesus' relationship with us and how does that affect our relationship with him? Get the picture, this isn't really a brief discussion in the vestry.

All this involves pain, it's never easy to take your cosy preconceived notions and subject them to interrogation. It becomes torture to hang onto them, to feel them crumble into folly inside you. However, it is through that process that you are healed. You arrive at the other end of an essay having been through a journey of sorts, each one breaks you in order to rebuild you. It's a process perhaps of learning to distinguish whether the objects in your imagination really are the eyes of God or simply the glistening barrels of a sawn-off shotgun.

It is also learning that there is a point to pain. We're so spoilt in the West we expect to have pain-free lives, it's become a human right enshrined in the creeds of every drug company and in the eyes of every concerned onlooker. When somebody does die or we are abandoned by someone we love our response is usually anger: it's a very negative despair. It is in our response to pain that we perhaps reveal our true humanity and our true selves, confused, scared, gracious, giving. I'm not sure that pleasure demands a response at all, or perhaps we have become so hardened to it that at best it involves a forgetting of our pain, a denial of our dilemmas.

Christianity has been accused many times of being no more than a barbed death cult. That perhaps is unfair. Christ on the cross in agony embraces our agony. God's forgiving love does not depend on the death of Christ but it is exacted in it.

True love bears burdens, it's gritty stuff; if it was all hearts, flowers and Hollywood we would indeed be living in a Godless, loveless world. Have a nice day.

It's turned cold; the tree opposite my study window is slowly revealing its bones, the leaves cling on, boasting, glorious, golden, before they pirouette down to the concrete and lie dead in the rain. Yesterday we stood in a redundant church and watched a fifteenth-century low Mass. Apparently it was all very authentic. The entire forty-five minutes was in mumbled Latin; it was freezing and people just simply stood about exchanging opinions and scandal; this was apparently authentic as well. Here was another helping of the theological amateur dramatics society. The church was beautiful, it had been illuminated by one William Morris. The overall impression was that of being incarcerated in a pre-Raphaelite fruit bowl, but the air was damp. There were plaques on the wall commemorating the lives of the long-ago faithful. That was the saddest of all; it wasn't the crumbling plaster, it was all the spent work, exuberance and effort that had clearly failed. The redundant churches fund had placed a wobbly table at the back with an untidy collage of badly designed leaflets, paper imploring us to join up and care for our national heritage. Flicking through the visitors' book it seemed that most of the admirers were either Australians whose comments were meditative or Italians gushing *bellissimos*. God was there but we had left him long ago. Half way through the proceedings Poacher along with a disgruntled Methodist and myself snuck off for an authentic twentieth-century cappuccino; we just made it back in time for the discussion groups that followed.

We're in deep financial agony; the Vice Principal's wife has volunteered to escort us around Sainsbury's and instruct us on how to feed and clothe a family of six for under £100 a month. There is a serious dichotomy here: the cheapest producers are increasingly the most environmentally destructive. The church I feel should support the ventures on organic farming. It should seriously consider the ideas of ethical investment. The reality is I'm sure that living on a stipend there is simply no financial room for organic tomatoes.

The ethics lecturer must have the last original late Sixties black crushed velvet jacket left in the Western world. I have never seen a man sit so still. He looks like a cross between a Pilgrim Father and Frank Zappa. I watched him intermittently through a lecture given by an eminently eloquent Lutheran Bishop. I must buy some of his coffee.

It's done, my brain has been forced through the food blender again. Doctrine essay number two is wrapped in the traditional plastic folder waiting to be marked. I always feel like I've chopped an entire shed full of logs after these essays. Their glow does come back to remind you of the sweat and grief involved in taking an axe to the bubbles of the theology in the wondrous cross.

I'm becoming increasingly haunted by the thought of actually having to try and make some sense of the reality of God and Christ as a curate. I always remember being told by a doctor that diagnosing a patient was like informed gambling: the patient could give you a few tips but at the end of the day you had to back your instincts. Looking for God is perhaps similar to that. Our relationship with him is deeply personal, it has to be if he cares on an individual basis, which is one thing I am certain about. However there are many questions, it's impossible to make sense of a painful death or senseless suffering simply because Christ's suffering was not senseless. There can be no standard answers, no platitudes, when a child has lost a parent or a parent has lost a child. However I have to believe in a God that bears the loss and that the cries of the wounded and dying soldiers are the cries of Christ on the cross. The alternative is angry oblivion; we can shake our fists at God but imagine the world if we accepted him and then blamed him for everything that went wrong. Life would be worthless, we'd be in bondage to hate. Sooner or later as an ordinand you have to give up your freedom of the world; you have to become bound by love and it has to be your choice. It's not an easy choice, it's not a comfortable choice, it is not possible to hold on to many of the values of society. There is a feeling that if you let them go you will lose touch with reality. I think you have to, you have to go with it.

I found myself speaking in tongues on Thursday. I wasn't aware of starting, I was just aware that my tongue was almost involuntarily exploring my mouth at great speed. I have no idea where it will lead me, however, I do know without a doubt that it's unforgettable now. I'm not the most holy of men, believe you me, and I cannot make sense of it other than that it feels utterly natural, it feels so totally gentle. I didn't pray for it, ask for it even, it appears to be something that has been switched on inside me. I haven't told anybody; I don't think it's the sort of information that gets blurted about, there's no need, no compulsion to tell anyone. It was just something I didn't ever associate with myself. I have always considered myself to be overflowing with sin, I smoke, I drink, I fall in love on the bus, I'm as vain as Narcissus and then this; it's thrown me completely.

It's been very cold lately, the sun arrives in the morning filtered by the mist, warming the white frost slowly. This is the most sensuous city I have ever lived in, it breathes secrecy. The ghosts of its history whisper to you continuously.

November 1993

Poacher has just landed a job down in Cornwall. His family are from Devon, his brother and his father are vicars down there. His father's retired now. So he's really going home. He used to be a tree surgeon but he's done many other things. After a spell as a Charismatic Evangelical he needed a psychotherapist for a year and naturally left the arms of the church. He spent some time on Dartmoor, he lived with a woman who was ten years older than him who by all accounts helped him a great deal. He is a most beautiful man.

The crash on the M40 motorway is another tragedy to join the list of this year: what can you say to the parents of those children? Their grief must be beyond words. I saw the headmaster crying on television. What a terrible loss. These things don't happen to us, do they? They always happen to other people. The sense of bewilderment and anger must be immense when something so senseless happens to somebody you love. Wounds like that take many years to heal; we're all unwilling to face the pain, to work it through, and it pursues us with its dreadful reminders of what's been lost.

People's lives do fall apart when they have to deal with pain like that. We spend a lot of time erecting pain insurance around ourselves, it's all useless; all we do is end up by denying it, by denying its existence and in the end we deny ourselves by denying our own feelings; it turns us into its slaves. Our actions are increasingly governed by keeping the pain we feel at bay: we become powerless in the process, life becomes a defence from feeling.

The decision to stop torturing yourself is a hard one to bear: it involves forgiveness, by forgiving the cause of pain you can begin to let it go. It was Christ who showed us not how to do it but how to live it, he simply accepted pain totally.

The party on F staircase was everything a theological college party should be: the crisps ran out five minutes after it started, the sound system left you feeling that you'd been mauled by a lawn mower, it inadvertently set the fire alarm off which set the house manager off and most of the married men left when two single and extremely gorgeous female Swedish language students arrived. It must have been the first time in their lives that men actually left the room they were in because they couldn't bear the sight of them. Sexual desire and Christianity are unhappy in the same bed, publicly at least. I was told a great story by the bald psychiatrist. Two Buddhist monks came to a river where there was a young woman unable to cross because of the current. One of the Buddhist monks offered to carry the young woman across on his back and duly did so, putting her down on the other side. The other monk crossed and the two monks set off again in silence. Five miles later the monk who hadn't carried the young woman said to the one that had, 'Doesn't it worry you having carried that woman over the river knowing that our vows do not permit us to have any physical contact with women whatsoever?'

'Ah,' said the other monk, 'I put her down five miles ago, it is you who are carrying her now.'

I'm more and more convinced the bald psychiatrist spent a previous existence as a bit actor in one of those old Elizabeth Taylor and Richard Burton Cleopatra movies: there's always a eunuch in the background isn't there, working the fan? Well, that's him.

It's been very cold and to my daughter's delight we've had some snow. She stood naked in front of an iced window, her body leaping with the shock of the white view, her words exploding jumbled sounds, spluttering sparks of excitement, melting the morning.

There's a former Telecom engineer at college; he's got sunny blue eyes, they usually clash with his shirts that more often than not look like they've been hewn from offcuts of his grandmother's curtains. He's a confirmed Derby County supporter. He organizes the football; he was the one who dropped me for dissent. Anyway, his study is opposite the other social secretary who's taken to subverting his carefully crafted essays in his absence. By the time serious sentences which start 'Calvin tried to reiterate the doctrine of redemption by etc. etc.' reach the attentions of the church history lecturer's pen they have been subtly transformed to read, 'Calvin, who was partial to the odd pint of lager, tried to etc.' The jousting continues on that front.

My wife is working again; she's producing a commercial for some nicotine patches to encourage people to stop smoking. The strain of it all has had the opposite effect. She's back on the fags, smoking for England. This means that I've been excused morning Chapel and all other services except the regular Sunday ones.

The Principal collared me after lunch in the common room where this year's crop of stoles and cassocks decorated with Noel Edmonds colour coordination hung empty on rails against a wall.

He said he'd had a letter about me. Apparently there was a retired Archdeacon in the congregation that I was preaching to on Sunday and he had been moved to write to the Principal saying how much he enjoyed my sermon. I think he must have been very old.

Yesterday due to the financial crisis I took off all my clothes and posed for a life drawing class in a scout hut not far from here. At least the Girl Guides who use the hut didn't get their dates mixed up. Just imagine, the press would have a field day, 'Trainee vicar strips for Girl Guides'. Have you ever considered that tabloids rhymes with haemorrhoids?

Theology and practise of ministry revealed to us this morning that 300 people are joining the church every week. This is good news, well it would be if 900 people were not leaving it every week, mostly through dying it has to be said, not of boredom, that was left unsaid.

We're in the open season on curacies now. Poacher, who was accepted for a job in Devon, has had the offer withdrawn. In the course of events he had an interview with the Suffragan Bishop and this is where things obviously started to go amiss. It's a torrid tale. Poacher had a nervous breakdown eight years ago. This was all open and discussed when he was selected for training. The Suffragan Bishop has somehow got hold of some information, nobody knows what it is because he will not say either what the information is or where he got it from, however, it's felt it's more than likely to be about the nervous breakdown and in the morning's post came a retraction of the job offer, not from the Suffragan Bishop but from the incumbent. These were most of his reasons: he felt it was a long way to move. He felt that as Poacher's wife was expecting their first baby, a move so far away from her parents and to an area where she did not know anyone would be ill advised. The letter ended with a rather cryptic note suggesting that Poacher ought to be trained by a more senior clergy pastor.

Is this what really happened? Somehow the Suffragan Bishop found out about the nervous breakdown. He obviously felt because this hadn't been discussed with himself or the training vicar that Poacher was trying to hide the fact from them. The Suffragan Bishop then quite clearly 'got at' the training vicar who then wrote the rather pathetic letter retracting the offer of the job.

I was under the impression that as Christians we had healing in Christ. What's more worrying is the level of intrigue, deceit and dishonesty that opens up when you scratch the surface here. The vicar concerned obviously chose not to stick his neck out and stand by his original decision. What a mess.

Here we have an institution that clearly cites God as the *raison d'être* for its own existence; when that institution behaves in an underhand and dishonest fashion the public will lose confidence in it. The church historically has had more than its fair share of double dealing, double standards and quiet corruption. That too is part of the legacy of the church along with its saints. Now all of these things can be neatly swept under the carpet in an authoritarian society. Authority has an honourable tradition in behaving in its own interests. However, with the onset of a pluralist society and the rise of the media the church has lost its establishment protector, it has been rumbled as being largely irrelevant and publicly imperfect.

The publicly imperfect bit wouldn't have mattered so much if since time immemorial it hadn't presented itself as being perfect, hadn't allowed its aspirations to dictate its image, hadn't sat above humanity rather than sat with it. I have met some of the most arrogant and intolerant people in my life since coming to theological college; I have also met some of the most intelligent and beautiful people. The arrogant and intolerant believe that God is on their side, that that belief entitles them to dictate the Jesus of faith who, not surprisingly, turns out to be a carbon copy of their own expectations. Belief becomes a system of belief, prayer becomes a justification of that system and the Bible becomes the rule book, a tool of suppression. Grace becomes measurable, predictable, it has certain colours, is spawned by certain beliefs. What have we done? What have we done to the immeasurable love of Christ; what are we doing to humanity, and why are we selling the Holy Spirit as a product of the church, something that's only available to those who turn up on Sunday? We must enable people whoever they are to seek God, not disable them in the process. The public aren't stupid, they can see the credibility gap when a church on crutches instructs people how to walk through their own lives. We do not own the Holy Grail. We have for too long believed that we do.

I've got the flu, sniffing, shaking, all very sobering really. All the really bad flu apparently comes from Beijing; are we sure this is not merely an MI5 plot to get us to distrust the Chinese and that this flu didn't actually emerge in Runcorn? I wonder what they call it in China. American flu, perhaps?

My wife has been away for three nights shooting the nicotine commercial. Being a single parent is not easy. It's given me an insight into what my mother had to go through.

I've reached the conclusion that I cannot allow myself to get depressed and angry about the church. The real trouble is that it's sick with conformity, mad with it almost. The main problem I think is that too many of the clergy have never known a professional way of working. The vast majority of them arrive at theological college steeped in Christianity and the church. Many of them have never known success, seen how the things they rely on such as fund-raising, public relations and property management are done properly. It's now almost certain that the church will be unable to pay people's stipends (salaries) sometime within the next twenty years. This is largely due to having to pay out ever-increasing sums in pensions. It's also due to massive ineptitude and failure on a scale that hardly bears thinking about. The standard answer I hear all the time at theological college is that we must 'empower' the laity. That the church must encourage its members to take responsibility for themselves, especially in rural areas. However this really side-steps the issue of its future, to reach the public in a meaningful way. Unless the church is able to face up to why it has had to close so many churches not to mention theological colleges, and why 600 people are leaving the church every week, this grand empowerment of the laity will really serve no other purpose than to implicate them in the demise of the church.

Can we really justify asking people to prop up an ailing institution without ever addressing the reasons as to why it's ailing in the first place? It becomes more and more apparent that we need some radical new ideas and a radical restructuring of the church itself. In my opinion it is quite pointless asking the establishment of the church to do this since it's plainly obvious that the very act of grabbing the bull by the horns would involve admitting failure and their own complicity in it.

I wish I could say I felt confident that my generation are prepared, armed and ready to take on this task, because we will most certainly have to, but since the workings of the Church of England are kept from us, since we are not schooled in where the church gets its money from and what it does with it, and because we are all being trained as model vicars, I'm not convinced that when shit comes to bust any of us will know what's happening and why. You're in serious trouble when you're wondering how many fish you've managed to catch if you don't realize your boat is sinking.

If you allow yourself to get depressed by all this then you're done for. Above all of this institutional suet must stand faith and the love of Christ. The institution of the church in a sense cannot really make a difference to that. At the end of the day it's why I'm here and at the end of the day it matters far more, is far far bigger than the ineptitude of the church that promotes it.

There are without doubt some very difficult times ahead. I'm quite sure we're destined for the wilderness but there is poetry and justice in that. I am not afraid. We perhaps need to re-focus: we will never know where we went wrong and why until we do so, and we can only ever have the strength to do that with Christ by our side.

I saw Brian Keenan, one of the Beirut hostages, on the box the other night. Towards the end of his reciting very eloquently the journey of his experience, he talked about prayer. He ventured inwards in solitude and what he found was an infinite vastness, with his Irish accent serenading the images of the wind-swept reaches of wild Ireland. You could see that he didn't so much come home, that perhaps was an impossible thing to do, but more he was looking at the landscape for the first time and almost within his voice you could feel the shock of that. The shock of what he saw, having touched the depths of the infinite vastness. What amazed me most was that he wasn't bitter. I cannot say whether he feels he has gained anything. He talked about a belief in personal freedom. I would imagine he would understand that notion more than most people.

I've made a stand on the mission; I've refused to go on it. I had a half-hour conversation on the phone with the pastoral studies tutor who basically said, at one point, that this act raised serious questions about my suitability for ministry. I had to do it. We live in an age cluttered by the media; people now communicate ideas, images, emotions through a myriad of avenues. I can see no point in fifteen people spending ten days knocking on doors in a rural Suffolk parish if at the other end of the scale everyone behind those doors thinks the church has nothing of relevance to say. We cannot address the micro level unless we also address the macro level and we do one at the expense of the other: there needs to be a balance. It's no wonder the church is failing to communicate the love of Christ if it adopts the same sales techniques as those selling fridge magnets and dodgy ironing board covers. I also said I was not prepared to leave my wife alone for ten days with our two young children but that really was a side issue. The pastoral studies tutor suggested she came with me. My pastoral studies tutor does not have two young children.

The next morning my personal tutor piled into our study with 'Can I have a word?' etched into his eyebrows. I was braced for a firm but polite mammoth rant which very surprisingly didn't materialize. Quite the reverse in fact. Although I'd left it all a bit late, because I had failed to write anything in my diary, this was a 'hot issue' and I was going to have to be as wise as a serpent. I was also urged very strongly to make this an issue about my family and encouraged to take a stand on my reluctance to leave them. This I said I couldn't do because if I felt that the situation demanded it I would leave them, albeit reluctantly and I stood by my micro, macro, fridge magnets, ironing board cover argument. Fate would have it that there was a staff meeting in the afternoon where this issue would be discussed. It was and I don't have to go. The Principal and I are going to put our heads together and come up with an alternative.

Behind this, of course, is something I am unsure about. I'm more and more convinced that people are encouraged to join the church as an end in itself and that in doing so they move from the enclosure of their lives into the enclosure of the church. All they do is exchange one set of principles for another; if that change was positive its effects would be there for all to see, but reality would dictate that this is not the case. We are losing the argument precisely because of our willingness to offer standard answers which result in standard lifestyles which affect nobody. The Church of England is so concerned not to rock the boat that everybody has fallen asleep.

Christians still troop out on a Monday morning and buy products which are suffocating and poisoning the world. They still exist in a consumer system that in the West uses supermodels to murder the rest of us by smiling. Christians still go to work in a business community that depends on the exploitation of either our environment or those paid the slave wages of the third world. In that context becoming a Christian is a purely selfish act, so that you may be saved from the ravages committed out of perceived necessity by your own hand. It's a sham. I believe most people in the rural Suffolk parish know it too. Unless the church is willing to deal on those terms with those issues, it can go on trotting out as many thoughts for the day as it likes, but it will go down because it ultimately won't be making any difference to anybody.

December 1993

Well, it's over: two terms to go. We had the review last night. The carol service and the meal were a quieter affair than the previous year. There were a few rogue table mats but it certainly wasn't the reincarnation of the previous year's glorious abandon. There was a motley collection of acts at the review. Maggi Dawn was very good; she's a singer songwriter who's had a lot of her work published in various modern hymn books as well as on the black plastic. The doctrine lecturer, the one without any hair, was press-ganged into performing as a fascist totalitarian skinhead with the bald psychotherapist and another ordinand who has the Kojak cut. The plot centred on the failure of the church in 2007. Lambeth Palace had resorted to the BNP to get its message into the hearts and minds of the population. It's strange how the most beautiful people make the ugliest faces. I was flapping around like a snipe on drugs backstage. One of my more memorable tasks was forcing a sixteen-stone skinhead into some ten-and-a-half-stone jeans.

Once again we'd asked people to vote for various categories. The Domestic Bursar came in for a lot of stick for his instigation of task forces which basically consist of small groups of ordinands acting as enforced labour filling in potholes, mending the plumbing and cleaning out the bird boxes. I actually think it's a very good idea; anyway he was unanimously cast as the Sheriff of Nottingham in a 'cast your own pantomime' section. The Principal once again took a great deal on the chin for his unusual clothes sense.

By and large it's been a dog of a term. My essays seem to have improved. I've managed credits for all of them so far; however, that has sadly been at the expense of my footballing performance which at best resembled the efforts of Long John Silver. But it's really been the full blown disenchantment with the Establishment of the Church that has hurt, the morbidity of the coffee and kittens culture and the realization that we've allowed consumer society to run off with and define our imagination. The shambles of the hunt for a curacy, and the moral corruption and weakness within the church that seems singularly unable to challenge the paranoid greed and environmental and spiritual genocide that we're all being told is progress.

The Evangelical response, of power breakfasts, polyester ties and the application of Eighties' management models, which packs churches with model Evangelicals saving the world from people like themselves, is equally disturbing. We desperately need new visions, a vision that faces the future, a vision that embraces the sickness and dullness of consumer society that is slowly murdering the humanity in all of us. A vision that looks outward into the streets, into the gutters, a vision that embraces our poisoned rivers, our addiction to materialism and our tragic reliance on interest rates to define our mental well-being. A vision that understands that loving your neighbour as yourself has the most massive implications in the context of the global village we all now live in. I am optimistic for the future, precisely because Christians have always expressed themselves better on their knees.

I have no doubt that the Evangelicals will grow in confidence and influence; they have their eyes on the prize of power. The rest of the church is so disorganized they won't be able to stop them. The Evangelicals are ultra-organized and, worst of all, they believe they are right. Groups such as 'Reform', which is against the ordination of women and also very unwilling to support the small less successful churches who do not hold its views, are without doubt in the ascendant. I admire immensely the preaching and honesty of the Evangelical tradition; however, and most dangerously, it lacks apologetics, it is judgmental and colourless; we need each other to balance out our extremes. It's hardly surprising that extreme positions are emerging. The die-off the Church of England is facing has, in a sense, distilled people's beliefs so instead of a sea of belief we are left with various unconnected ideological puddles each furiously building dams around themselves in the vain attempt to stop any more water loss. What they seem to have forgotten is that they don't own the water, which leaves them as sole proprietors of the wall which they have erected around it.

It's one of those cold light blue winter days. There's a very white square oblong which rises above the jumble of roofs.

Next to it there is a silver chimney burnt in the sunlight. It's only England because I think it is; it could be anywhere.

The press seem to be enjoying themselves. On Sunday they were cackling about disestablishment and today it's mumbling over the possibility of the existence of hell. The Principal is in the thick of it, quoted as 'the principal of a theological college'. He agrees with the Bishop of Durham that it is inconceivable that a God of love would wish to torture humanity indefinitely. I very much liked Hugh Montifiore's version: although it read like a British Rail timetable, it did arrive at the conclusion that it was humanity's volunteered separation from God that was hell. And that there is always the possibility that we will all be loved into heaven, that God's love never gives up and therefore is constant. Anyway tomorrow it will be yesterday's news and by then we'll all be craving another hit from a new sensation.

It's three days before Christmas; even the hypes have been hyped. London was dull and dirty; the advertising hoardings appear to have relegated all sense of creative selling into the past. They bawl mediocracy. It is clear that our great dream of a liberal democracy has become no more than a labour camp of consumerism, hence the joyless posters.

I was on my way back from seeing a possible title; it all looks a lot more promising than the dreadful first two and the not quite right third one. It's an Anglo-Catholic parish. I'm very keen to experience as many different traditions as possible, partly so they can't turn around and bite me and partly so that I don't get sucked into any of them and end up worshipping the traditional rather than God and having a pair of spectacles imposed on me that I can never remove.

He was a quiet man, a doctor, I didn't ask him what in, but I think there was an understanding that we perhaps needed each other. The last incumbent had left the church over the ordination of women. I think and hope we got over that one. He quite clearly has serious reservations about it and I do not. But what I felt was important was that we worked together; no stigmatism, no more hurt, it's caused enough of that. Anyway we agreed to speak after Christmas as to whether or not we should continue the dialogue. I received a very frank and open letter from the Bishop of Southwark expressing his concern over the way that my wife had indirectly been treated. So that has calmed the waters somewhat; it's a terrifying prospect though if any of that lot ever become Bishops, it may well be me that goes after that, or do you stand and fight? Stand and fight.

The Bishop of Durham's done it again: it's all over for the three wise men. Personally I think he's doing a great job. Christmas surely isn't actually about the three wise men, it's about the birth of Christ and if we content ourselves with pretty pictures, allow ourselves to wallow in the symbolism then that's as far as we'll get. I have a sneaking suspicion Dr Jenkins is trying to push us past all that into the really deep water. If that means popping a few armbands on the way so be it.

January 1994

Well we're back: it was a particularly cold day, the sky throwing rain over everything. The river hasn't burst yet but it looks very full. To think that in Australia they're fighting the worst fires for fifty years, fanned by hot winds; it could almost be another planet looking out of this window. The main topic of conversation after the hall meeting which was more of a formality than anything else was the Archbishop of Canterbury's excursion into the Sudan. No one seemed too perturbed that the Sudanese have expelled our Ambassador and the Prime Minister has reciprocated by expelling theirs. The main thrust of the discussion seemed to centre around the Archbishop's hat. I must agree what on the face of things appeared to be some quite good media coverage for the ecclesiastical corner was badly flawed by the hat in question. It really looked as though he'd actually forgotten his hat and a sympathetic Christian Sudanese baker had simply thrown a circular lump of dough on to his head. I can only assume he quite simply forgot he was walking around the Sudanese bush sporting what resembled an uncooked pizza base. Whether he'll insist on wearing it to the next Arsenal game remains to be seen. What the media didn't report was that in one particular village the Archbishop was given a crucifix made out of used gun cartridges. He was holding this crucifix aloft whilst speaking about peace and a dove landed on it as he was talking.

I've mapped out a timetable for all my remaining work which is non stop from here until 1 June—six months solid unmitigated theological blitz.

I have another sermon to preach next Sunday. This is the one where they all come and listen and where we pull it to pieces afterwards. We all went down to Devon over the New Year. It's a very wild place, North Devon; it's utterly beautiful. There was a gale on our second night rattling the windows. It was so fierce, so uncompromising, it took down all the rotting trees. We're far too polite in the church and it's politeness that has in turn domesticated Christ. If he is the calm then he is also the storm, there cannot be one without the other.

Theological college can be very painful; having all you hold true mercilessly kicked by academic boots is bruising, but it needs to happen. The process cannot be made painless simply because we want it to be.

Within this mayhem I have recently felt a great sense of overwhelming wellbeing. It is disturbing because there is no reason for it. I have been preparing for an ethics essay and have read some really quite remarkable passages, not least of which is C.S. Lewis' *Mere Christianity*. But the one that just exploded off the page was written by Oliver O'Donovan. He wrote, 'It was the mark of Christ that so far from overthrowing the given order of things he rescued it from the emptiness into which it had fallen.' No violence, no trickery, no bribery. How did he do it? It is such a beautiful and terrifying prospect that our world perception, our striving against loneliness is focused on a murdered carpenter's son. And yet this divine madness still persists. The rain is falling outside; it could be sand against the window. Words are so easy, they spill and get lost, however I do not believe that one drop of water is wasted in the same way. There is so much I take for granted, every moment is given, born of love, we're a long way from home.

We've done the youth course. Two very youthy blokes turned up wearing different coloured laces in their shoes, and told us how to insure a minibus for an hour and a half, but before then we experienced the '101 things to do with a parachute' session, followed by half an hour venting your frustration in a game of indoor hockey. It's all been rather confusing; the main thing that comes across from all these short courses is that each special interest group has its own needs: toddlers, children, adolescents, teenagers; the list is endless and it can be broken down still further. We are of course always dealing with individuals; to put people into a group is perhaps the first mistake. There may be certain platitudes that might hold water for a minute or two but they are very fragile things.

Today was the church and the media. A real hot potato. We had to write a thought for the day which was then recorded and discussed: mine was on the consummate perfection of Torville and Dean. We were then all instructed on how to write a press release, a very useful skill. However, the disagreements started over the strategy. Imagine if we all became expert at writing press releases, as someone commented. Every weekend there would be the usual diet of 4,000 Jumble Sales, 3,000 Bring and Buy sessions, and sixteen vicars abseiling off their respective steeples. This would soon lose its appeal. In the absence of a strategy what are all these press releases for? Most of the activities of the church just confirm its Christmas card image. It's not that the local media shouldn't know, it's just that we maybe need to be more creative about what we do. I would recommend campaign periods which are national: rolling yearly programmes which look at marriage one year, homelessness the next and so on. This would give the church a much needed point of reference with society.

Well, we're all off and running again. I'm not sure I managed to set off for 20 March on the B of the Bang. But lectures started today. I've opted for a course of resurrection pills: these are delivered every Thursday morning. I'm hoping they'll have an accumulative effect. The first dose simply obliterated the fatigue bacteria which had crept in over the year. We are actually all guinea pigs. This course is new, virgin territory if you like, free from hobnail prodding and sharp little theological minds dissecting the words.

The short courses came to a rather flat end. The media course was good, more bones than flesh. Our thoughts for the day were recorded by a crew of women religious journalists. They were far too polite, much too nice. The assembled styles numbered from a sort of high-pitched Listen with Mother right through to Norman Lamont after the red wine. The most frightening thing was that we all sounded like vicars: well-meaning, uninspiring and half dead. Christianity, as the programme controller of Anglia Television argued, is suffering from a creative crisis. He barnstormed a meeting we all attended in Norwich and in short reaffirmed the fact that Christians had lost more of the airtime on radio and television because the programmes were so dreadful. And if we put out material like 'Highway' under the assumption that people will want to watch it, we need a psychologist, not God.

The course on ageing didn't seem as great a success as it was last year. I met the woman who was taking it in the post room and she said most people knew more about it than she did. I wasn't sure whether that was a satirical comment on the mental age of Church of England ordinands or the fact that she was under siege from a battalion of experienced counsellors in senile dementia. One of the more uncompromising of our number who was attending the course failed to turn up for the third day, saying she was suffering from rigor mortis. I've been up to my neck writing a sermon for this Sunday. This is the scoring Sunday when the others in my preaching group along with the Principal have to suffer my efforts. I'm taking morning prayers tomorrow and leading the communion service on Thursday, planning staircase prayers on Monday and there is an ethics essay due in on Tuesday. I'd better start running.

What a week. It's Friday. This evening we all shoot off down to Guildford for the weekend interview. It goes like this: Lunch with the vicar 12.30. Dinner with the churchwarden that evening. Sunday services then lunch with the other churchwarden on Sunday. Free food. We had a long protracted debate last night over whether partners should be put through these gruelling sessions. I have to say I think not. However, this is a difficult point. Whatever is said to the contrary your partner, Christian, Buddhist, Born-again Biker, is definitely given the once over. That's all fine if they want to throw themselves into the parish, running Bible classes, taking services, whatever. If they are not of that persuasion then why are they going? Fair enough if you are offered the job, but otherwise what's it all for?

It's been a very good week. The second ethics essay is just about done and dusted but the high points were really the return to doctrine and the Eucharist last night. The return to doctrine was as mind blowing as ever. This was followed this morning by a worship class on exorcism and the realm of demons. It increasingly seems to me that we're all in danger of seeing the God we want to see. What do we see? Our ideas of God? Or God's ideas about us? Historically the church has been about its own ideas about God. This is tidy and neat on the one hand because you can rattle out the party line, but it's utterly useless on the other hand because you can rattle out the party line. In theory the church can never really change, it is static, it is our ideas about God that alter it; it is clearly our ideas about God that also change and these usually come up against the fabric of the church and the Establishment who would far rather things stayed as they are. There is movement, tension, it's fair to say there always has been and, looking back through church history, the most exciting times seem to be aligned to the periods of greatest tension. We need tension: we need to recognize its creative qualities; when you're on the tightrope I imagine you concentrate pretty hard. But renewal movements have clearly come and gone. By gone I mean the revolutionaries have been absorbed into the Establishment. History travels secret paths leaving its remains on the landscape. We usually mistake them for reality whereas all they are is someone's vision about reality then. We can never have it. We spend most of our lives as tourists observing other people's attempts to put reality in a box or deny it completely. The great painters constantly remind us of this with the brilliance of their visions. The strength of their portrayal and the self-constructed fragility of the portrait remind us that to believe merely what we see simply puts us in a prison of our own making, and when we've taken that in we are free for a while.

The reality of God is utterly positive, there are no walls around it, there is a massive sense of incredible freedom and release. Christians always go bashing on about this but it is I think the hardest thing to explain. True Christianity enhances humanity, enhances your humanity. You are invited to look at the world again and your part in it. It takes a long time to begin to be able to recognize God's ideas about us, but the experience is like nothing I have ever felt before: it is so beautiful that I believe we only ever see glimpses of it: to feel the full force of it all the time would render us incoherent. We would not, I believe, be able to live here as we are. God seems to allow each of us the measure we can cope with. I believe Jesus Christ could manage the full reality of God and therefore it is not at all surprising he said what he said and did what he did. I happen to believe he was ordained by God to show us what that reality consisted of. I do not think that any human being could bear it for long, we are simply not strong enough.

The service yesterday evening briefly touched that reality. We all know it, felt it, and as the preacher said, it is always so close to all of us.

Well it's a pretty low day, to be honest. The church down in Guildford have said no to the curacy there. I'm not surprised and I don't blame them. It was a charade, the happy curate and his happy wife. Essentially they wanted someone who would agree with them and I didn't agree over the issue of the ordination of women. I wasn't going to pretend otherwise. The incumbent was great, very very good indeed. I agreed with Jacs that we wouldn't go through it again, not together. I don't think it's really fair since she has no designs on the role of curate's wife. But it's now pretty much the end of January and I don't see many curacies coming up outside London, so it's not only feeling bleak it's looking pretty bleak as well.

I have a major flaw in church terms and doubtless in myself and that is I'm not really worried about churchmanship. It seems to pervade everything like the way you speak, it's your accent and as we all have one, I too have a churchmanship, simply and, in my opinion, by default. The whole experience of looking for a curacy is not a pleasant one; character building it may be but it leaves you feeling as if you've failed. All I really did was fail to impress them down in Guildford. I'm not sure that I really should have been trying to do that in the first place, but when in Rome behave as the Romans. They must have spotted my barbarian heart and thought, wait a minute we have an interloper here; they did.

In the absence of a concrete future there is no choice but to trust in the will of God. I have a feeling that's what he wants, always more, always more.

We've just had the most furiously beautiful thunderstorm. The wind driving the rain upwards off the roofs, everything blowing in every direction at once; lightning freezing the flashing moments into my mind; I wish I could remember every one.

February 1994

The post mortem continues. I had a good half hour with the Principal. He can be a very perceptive man at times. There is nothing to worry about really. The bottom line is either a curacy comes up or it doesn't. I have no control over that and if we have to take a year out so be it. Most of the grief is created by my own impatience. I really want to get on with it. I spent so long denying my calling that I want to try and catch up. The system of looking for a curacy is shot to bits, it works by virtue of the fact that there is nothing else, but nobody loves it, nobody respects it, it has nobody's confidence and therefore people put it down to the will of God simply because no one can be bothered to make it work well. No wonder he gets such bad press.

My wife is getting a lot of verbal about the Church of England. It appears that everyone wants it to be something different; the only uniting factor is that everyone wants it to agree with them. Although Paul's passage about being fools for Christ is undoubtedly the truth of the matter I'm not sure whether he would have much truck with the notion that we should be perceived as being incompetent for Christ. There is obviously a great deal of interest about the church: once they find out who she's married to they do go on and on apparently, but it's all very negative. Our divisions are apparently egotistical and petty, but they do not see the soul-searching agony behind them. Shaking hands at the peace is viewed as being something very creepy, which means the whole notion of the body of Christ is a complete anathema. Charismatic worship, guitars and all, is apparently certifiably insane and I would imagine unless the gifts of the Spirit are sensitively explained it must look that way. In short the church has become a negative option.

I don't think we can plough ahead with our own lives and watertight agendas. If we are failing the people of this country we are failing them for a reason. I don't support a public relations exercise either, it's utterly worthless under the circumstances; papering over the cracks will not stop the rot eating away at the plaster underneath. We really do have to ask some hard questions about our faith and more importantly the expectations of it. We have clearly gone wrong somewhere. I'm not convinced that a quick hit from the Charismatics will put everything right, our troubles are far too deep for that. Our prayers are made of paper, they cost nothing; they seem to be a jumble of requests of things we want, advertising the flavour of the month, which come Monday morning is forgotten along with the beautifully crafted sermons and moving hymns.

We have lost our way, there is no pattern, no suffering Christianity, there is so much talk about the material poverty of the church, no one has said anything about our spiritual poverty. Our reliance on books has fed our brains to bursting point; we have so much knowledge of other people's ideas and their prognosis of other people's ideas. In college we have one hour quiet time a week, but everyone is under so much pressure to deliver this essay, organize that service that it goes by the wayside. We have no spiritual instruction at all. There is no spiritual discipline to speak of. How can we teach others if we have never been taught ourselves? How can we say the Holy Spirit will heal you, hear you, if we are not taught to listen, to recognize the voice? We end up with a system of religion that recognizes the grace of God as an idea; most of us worship the idea and have no grasp whatsoever about the terrifying reality.

Why do we want everything to be so logical, understandable? Every time we pin God down we make him smaller. We are caught in this negative game. Surely if we believe we have nothing to prove, nothing at all, we have sacrificed faith for reason.

The doctrine of the incarnation is an idea. The beauty of holiness is an idea. The Bible containing the word of God is an idea. Apostolic succession is an idea. So we leave college with all these ideas, they're not rooted in anything except other people's ideas. We are asked to absorb them. Surely if we believe, we have nothing else to prove. Most of us will leave and give off our own ideas to other people; not our experience not our quiet reconciliation to God, but our ideas about him. The love of God is fluid, the reality of the Holy Spirit is a constant, it's moving, it's alive, the rest is our invention.

We had a seminar class yesterday afternoon in the Principal's study to dissect the efforts of another member of the sermon syndicate. We picked over the bones of what I had had to say last week, it was unanimously agreed that I was trying to squeeze four sermons into one; it certainly felt like it at the time. I really don't like pulpits, they are lonely places. This week's victim had the unfortunate task of preaching on the Antichrist. In fact the church timetable billed the event as 'Simon Cawdell—the Antichrist'. I would have expected the title to draw some huge crowds but it didn't: there must have been about twenty-five of us loosely squeezed into a church built for several hundred.

Before we all set about dissecting his efforts he informed us about the context. That is to say the state of the individual church: what a mess. There was an area of broken relationships, bitterness and politics into which he simply couldn't go without the real prospect of making things worse.

I'm convinced our churches have become fortresses, places where the outside world is kept at bay and the truth is protected from the marauding media, hostile politicians and a disaffected population. But what are we guarding, what are we protecting? The more we act as owners of the body of Christ, the more entry requirements we insist upon for the Kingdom of Heaven, the more broken we seem to become. What we're left with is a chain of run-down cinemas showing the same film; the public stroll in and out occasionally to see their favourite bits and to be told that unless they put their hands in their pockets the cinema will close. We're fighting to maintain the churches, the institution. It's a pointless battle that we will lose. I can't imagine anything worse than spending my life propping up the masonry. It's not bloody well working. The model of ministry needs to change or at least needs to diversify radically. Our model of the house of God is holding us back. The idea that churches are holy places simply means that offices, night-clubs, factories and farms are not. The idea of consecrated ground means that the rest of the land is unconsecrated. If this is God's world then all of it is holy, every atom. We can see his anger when we destroy one of those.

The parish system has become almost unworkable because people simply do not view their locality as their world. The media has put live San Francisco in everybody's homes, the result has been a massive explosion of our symbolic universe; the world has got bigger, and as a consequence the church has got smaller. Relationships cross continents, let alone parish boundaries; we are touched by people's hands who pick the oranges we eat, those who make the cars we drive; this is something that is worldwide. The parish system was based on a flat worldview. I'm sure this must have been said before but it's way past its sell-by date. The Church of England will be viewed as a relic from the past if it's structured on those terms. If people have lost confidence in the system, church people and public alike, then it needs changing. It's as simple as that. The management of the church is an utter shambles; I think it is a miracle in itself that so many people have suffered it for so long.

I went to see a parish on Friday. It's rural, very rural. The vicar was great; he must have been late forties, early fifties, single, lives with his mother in the vicarage. I have to say it's much more my scene. His house was ramshackle. He must have had over a thousand classical LPs and it was easy. We'd be about three miles away in another village where there is a school; everyone seemed very friendly unlike the pink Dralon spikies of a couple of weeks ago. I spoke to him this evening and I've got to meet the Bishop now; it's rather like a glorified game of snakes and ladders, so it's back to the pub for the lowdown on what not to mention. So much for my stance on fairness. All this has come through the ecclesiastic equivalent of the old boy network, the 'dear boy' network. I should have made a stand: I should really refuse to go by any route except the one provided by the system but in time-honoured fashion it's clearly who you know not what you know. I can rightly be accused of running with the hare and hunting with the hounds. But I am sadly resigned to the fact that this regrettable option is a good deal more appealing than placing myself into the hands of the bishop who is meant to organize a clearing list of jobs that was due in three weeks ago. Would you entrust your future to someone called Barry Bristol?

We spent the weekend down in Newham, East London, in a multi-cultural church centre learning about Christian multi-cultural worship with one Patrick Sookhdeo, a Muslim convert Christian vicar. He didn't pull his punches, he got stuck in right from the bell. He's clearly an exceptional man. We were taken to Green Street Market for a blend of Caribbean vegetables, African-style and My Little Pony slippers, the colours and cultures haggling over your senses, the women in saris serene and always the hum of different tongues left in the jamboree of empty spaces. The minibus continued down Green Street, the driver interjecting stories of sweat shops against a line of Seventies English mannequins hiding behind the shop glass dressed to kill in the colours of Karachi.

In the afternoon we went to a church that stood almost alone in what looked like the tidy side of a bomb site. The vicar there had one of those travelled faces that resembled an ageing angel. He spoke quietly in the cold church, the stained-glass windows blackened by pollution, surrounded by vases of plastic flowers. The only interruption came when a boy daringly opened the door at the back, shouted 'tossers' and then ran out again. The vicar smiled as I'm sure an angel would and said that was an unusually mild rebuke and then carried on talking. He said he'd decided to take the job as it was likely to be his last but he also added that it was the hardest and the best thing he'd ever done and that his relationship with God had gone through the roof. There was an immense still sense of the Holy Spirit there and it was a privilege to meet him.

Back at the multicultural centre we were all inspired to fight racism. The racist shit Patrick Sookhdeo had to put up with at theological college back in the enlightened Sixties was shameful. He's fought them all, won some, lost some; he won't stop fighting, it's not in his nature. Sunday lunch was interesting: lasagne, shepherd's pie, curried rice, daal, chapatis and spicy peas, all on one plate. I'd forgotten just one of the morning's points and inadvertently touched the shoulder of the young Asian woman I was sitting next to; when I came back from a second helping she'd moved her chair away from me. The Pentecostal Church of Grace after lunch was guaranteed to inspire indigestion. We arrived at two, when we left at quarter past four the service was still going. It certainly puts church unity into perspective. They worship God with their hearts and their bodies. We tend to worship God with our minds, our hearts locked up behind reinforced Anglican reserve. It made the Church of England look like a golf club; the Peace took about fifteen minutes; the communion was flavoured with impressive Charismatic singing, sometimes in tongues, verses of the Bible swinging upwards into the rafters. I didn't want to leave when we did, I wanted to stay to the end but our schedule reigned supreme. We slipped out and were walked to our cars with grace and absolute dignity.

There's trouble at mill. There was an emergency Common Room meeting today, followed by a staff-student meeting. Things are at crisis point. Naturally it was diffused beautifully; we simply poured the Holy Spirit on troubled waters. The problem seems to be one of too much to do and no time to do anything else: every moment is accounted for. There were those who thought we needed to be a more vertical community; there were those who thought the students needed to be trusted; there were those who thought everything ought to be voluntary; and there were those who thought we ought to love one another. The staff thought this was all a good starting point, I thought the body language in the room would have entertained a psychoanalyst for hours. However the conclusion was we are victims of a driven community. The Evangelical work ethic makes the Protestant work ethic look like an afternoon tea party, and because all we do is work, everything else gets squeezed out, everything gets swallowed by the voracious appetites of excellence, competitiveness and perfection. Chapel becomes a function rather than a feeling. The mistakes we make become prey to perfection.

As it was rightly pointed out this is an argument about spirituality. The charge levelled at the functioning system is that the present is robbed of its meaning and significance to pay for this constant commuting to the past. Christ becomes the heroic figure whose message has to be dug out from between the lines of the letter to the Ephesians and no more. We end up with crossword Christianity, everybody buried brow-deep in books seeking the cryptic solution hidden in the small print of Paul. It is fascinating, mind-blowing at times, but when it becomes obsessive it does so at the expense of everything else. The ever-present Spirit of Christ becomes a logical conclusion rather than a staggering reality. We are useless without the still small voice of calm at the centre of our senses.

If we are listening to the words of prayer to spot the doctrine it will be unable to lift us to God. There is a recognition that as a driven community we perhaps have paid too much attention to the vehicle, not noticing that the landscape we are driving through had become barren and parched. We need rain. No one is getting on the Christian bus because they have mortgages to pay, mouths to feed. We need perhaps to move outwards from a spirit of love that's felt rather than thought. A love through Christ that is demonstrated through action to offer a balance to this dreadful consumerism which, as it is so aptly titled, consumes everything in its wake: our hearts, our minds, the air, the sea, the trees, everything. Not even a single snowflake in the distant Arctic or the serene flight of the furthest albatross is spared from the poisoned presence of this cancer of greed and materialism that has robbed us of our dignity and our true humanity.

The whole notion of the profit principle used as a justification for and the means of human existence is obscene. We have as a culture glorified theft. It's been packaged as giving services and servicing material needs but what we are really doing is no more than stealing off each other. It's not surprising that all of us are encouraged not to think beyond the supermarket shelf or our bank balance because we might for a moment stop thinking about ourselves and that would be very dangerous indeed. We might even start to love each other and that would be even more dangerous, catastrophic in fact for the current scheme of things.

When my wife's temperature reached 104 I called the doctor, he'd already been in the morning. Small, earnest, his moustache curling with common sense. Our new son as well has this dreadful virus, it's been three days in hell for all of us. She's up today, a little wobbly but the baby is not happy. We steamed the room last night because he simply couldn't stop coughing.

This afternoon I have a three-hour worship exam, everybody at college is running around desperately seeking assurance that nobody else has done any work for it either.

It's Valentine's Day; the post room this morning was packed. The Arch-Evangelical made a hasty exit clutching what appeared to be three pristine white envelopes, he definitely had the look of someone who was going to open his mail in private. Most of us settled for a passionate red-covered booklet that had been distributed to all and sundry titled *Training for Ministry: The Invaluable Handbook*. Not exactly an invitation to a romantic rendezvous in petal-strewn sheets.

My son was baptized on Sunday. I'm not sure whether the Soho contingent really grasped the spiritual nettle or exactly how many pints the features editor on the *Racing Post* had needed to calm his nerves before his godparent vows. I always get slightly worried about combining my previous life with my current one; it's rather like allowing someone to inspect the contents of your sock drawer, but they seemed to chug along together. At the end of the day my baptism policy was shot. My son was hopefully going to grow up in a vicarage with a strange father who occasionally took to wearing even stranger clothes and bursting into tears every time Maria came back from the nunnery in *The Sound of Music*: his godparents really ought to provide him with a balance. So representing the ecclesiastical corner we had Poacher who was sporting a particularly vitriolic Caribbean shirt, one godmother is from New Zealand, the other was an old flame and providing the ultimate balance was the features editor (half cut) of the *Racing Post*, who bears a passing resemblance to Mick Jagger.

We had snow this morning soothing the bare patches, hiding the wrinkles of the winter garden. We managed about three hours sleep last night. The doctor came over and said we should take him to hospital to be checked over and prodded again, basically he's been screaming for 36 hours. When they took off his clothes and laid him in the cot he beamed and gurgled at the paediatrician; the transformation was total. He loved the stethoscope, chewed the monitor attached to his finger and made eyes at the nurses; when we got him home he started crying again.

It's been a sobering day; I spent twenty minutes with my Pastoral Tutor who was immediately understanding. I don't have to do anything until Monday morning. Just to stop was wonderful; just to sit and look at the tall and empty trees through the study window was a lesson in itself. Our eyes deceive us. Normality confuses us into believing it's all normal; it isn't. The Holy Spirit lives in the spaces between us, is the glass we see everything through. We get vague reminders when the light catches the glass, worries our constructed reality encamped in our fortress of being. The poets, the writers, the musicians, have the gift perhaps of reminding us that our lives are built in the fortress. They tempt us out from time to time, our timid hands stretching to touch the leaves, our eyes, washed with tears, clear to marvel at the moment's glory. To dance in the land where God lives, intoxicated on nothing other than reality observed, daring to step into the present. The artists, poets, musicians show us: the clear river water, the torture of a violent death, the last breath, in them we perhaps see ourselves; the failing flowers, the timeless view that held our entirety, the utterly terrifying beauty of seeing the person we love naked, undress us.

We say we are taken out of ourselves by these experiences, we forget who we are. I tend to feel it makes us remember and it is moments such as these when perhaps we come closest to who we are, it is in those moments that we perhaps reach out and touch the Holy Spirit, when we are taken beyond our preconceptions to glimpse the potential of perfection, of our own perfection, and it's there in all of us.

When Christians speak of the presence of God what they are really saying is their presence in God's presence, that's what we experience. Our experience of ourselves in the presence of God is one of beauty; we experience our own beauty. That involves recognizing our wretchedness, our own poverty-stricken understanding of love. People die for this, they die because they will not and cannot reject that experience as false, as madness. We are scarred by the Holy Spirit only in the sense that we are shown our scars and we know that the bearing of those scars is the way to God. What makes Jesus Christ divine is that he needed no healing. He was the whole, is the 'I am'. He carried no baggage of time. To all those that met him I imagine he was the moment remembered. He had no need of our brittle reality. In being raised from the dead he showed us our reality for what it is and our grasp of the beauty and potential of love as always inadequate.

March 1994

I met the Bishop today. So much for Bishop's palaces, it was a 1940s double-fronted house, number 14. Number 13 looked exactly the same. He's one of those men whom you have no choice but to be honest with. Any attempt to impress, cajole, charm is doomed to failure. He told me that 'Yes,' he would definitely be prepared to ordain me. He didn't so much drop it in, it was more of a sentence on its own. It was followed by one of those pregnant delays where I fumbled for something suitable to say. I wasn't aware that this was a big decision, but apparently no one can be ordained unless they can actually find a bishop who is prepared to ordain them. We talked around a lot of things. Although he did make it quite clear that the church and faith appeared separate at the moment I agreed with enthusiasm. But there was no escaping his all consuming intelligence.

This morning as part of the social calendar twelve of us set out through the wilds on a ten-mile sponsored walk. The Arch-Evangelical had complained that sponsored walks were far from sound, citing 'Salvation by works'. I think what he's suggesting is that it's all right to sit up half the night planning the next Christ by numbers broadside to capture the hearts and minds of the unsuspecting public but he's not walking round the mulberry bush to do so.

There had been a heavy frost the night before and the morning was brilliant blue and utterly still. We walked across fields past quiet farmhouses, stopping for lunch in a pub, no one else came in, it was on the main road. We drank lager and ate platefuls of chips and tomato sauce. Fantastic. Then off again down along the edge of a large wood bordered by a stream, the sunlight packed into Picasso shadows slicing through the leafless trees. On the last hill two skylarks headed upwards, their song trembling with delight serenading the distance. The nomadic culture of infant Judaism surely marvelled at these things, lived the ecstasy, reached out into the breathing seam that sustains all life, reached inwards to recognize the dwelling of the same deep within humanity. It isn't the lark—it simply sang what we felt, sang what we saw. It wasn't a divine act in the sense that God ordered the lark upwards, it was a divine act because the lark was free to do what she did; she was singing 'I am' and there we touched; it is the only place we can meet, where we all meet, where everything meets.

It's been a very hard week. My wife and myself are still struggling with the hangover of not being well. Everything has taken more effort than normal. My old vicar sent me a clipping about himself which appeared in a London paper. The description of his sitting room is as follows: 'There is not a thing of beauty in the room and nearly everything is brown—the carpet, the piano, the furniture—dull Anglican brown. Trousers and socks are drying on a radiator. The oval clock above the mantelpiece has stopped.' The journalist was right, but it is the picture of the church the public want to have. With the failure of the Church Commissioners you can also sense a baying for blood. I now believe it is utterly futile expecting the Church of England to be any different. There is simply not the will or the vision for change. We will more than likely cling to the dead wood of the Established Church as it is swept on to the rocks because most of us believe that Christ is in the church. Christ was not mad about institutions. He defied their labels; all of humanity's attempts to pin him down were futile.

His spirit has proved equally resilient. Is he in the liturgy? the baptism? Church House? ordination? the Eucharist? are we going to sit around for another hundred years and argue the toss while the planet suffocates and starves? The training at theological college relies heavily on preparing people to be accountants, sexual therapists, psychotherapists, youth workers, bereavement councillors, liturgists, choirmasters, church historians. Is God there in any of these? Did the Apostle Peter need doctrine, was John trained in Office Management, was James instructed on how to plant a church? No, they relied on the Holy Spirit. They relied on God. Give me 50p, put me on the streets for a week. Show me the beauty of the mountains, the suffering of the children's ward, the hell of hatred, the dying mother. If my spirit does not respond, if the Holy Spirit doesn't tear my preconceptions to ribbons when confronted with reality, the reality we have constructed, if I am not moved to respond and comfortable and terrified with that movement then all I have is teaching, words, nothing else. The church is a dying institution. The Evangelicals may be able to pep it up for a bit, but it will die unless we abandon our ideas of God, our beautiful Taizé chants, our glorious Celtic spirituality; it's all meaningless. We need to see God in the present, respond in the present, not weighed down by the ballast of the past. We will not feel the breath of Christ by plotting a course that takes us to some faraway place. If Christ is in the present he is already in the future. How can we embrace him in the present if we are looking for him in the past? We will find his footprints perhaps, see the beauty he has born, the grace he has inspired, the martyred love in every faithful murder. But surely he calls us to the future, not to the past. He stands before us always. I will lead you, let me lead you. Too often we are safe where we are, we've gone far enough.

Our perpetual search for the Holy Grail, our yearning for the womb of history, the safe ground surrounded by the walls of human knowledge, keeps us from Christ. The calling of every generation is to make history, not to wallow in it. For Christians it is only possible in Christ, not the Christ that was, but the Christ that is. Because unless we can live as if Christ is, the I am is, we live in a land where he was; we won't find him there because he's here. Our churches are monuments to the past, cenotaphs full of dead names. We can no more serve them than Admiral Nelson. We will never find a living tradition in the arms of the dead. We need churches but we need people inside them more, whispering the secrets of the living Christ, not the words of a dead religion. History is our guarantee of sanity perhaps, that there is a living line of faith that stretches back to those who heard the sermon on the mount and believed, but does it urge us forward or back? We will perhaps find through it the basis of our own faith but not the basis of our being. Our human being breathes this air now, we cannot breathe it again. Those Evangelicals who urge us back into the New Testament households, back into the boat with Paul, use the Bible as a legal document, a rule book to imprison us all in the past. Yes, it's comfortable, even academically exciting, dissecting every word for more law, but it denies the present, renders it impotent, unimportant.

Our historical reliance on the past has meant we have been unable to embrace the present and dream of the future. It also in part denies the existence of Christ as present and all the terrifying beauties and reality that this consciousness entails. John Gummer has left for Rome. So far everyone has been terribly reasonable about it: there's been the stuff about one's own conscience. But in reality it's pretty shabby. I can't imagine he agrees with everything the Tory party does so it would appear that politics has nothing to do with conscience, no surprises on that front. I find it incredulous that he seems more than willing to sanction the building of a nuclear reprocessing plant, which by the Government's own admission is destined to kill over 2,000 people; be hauled into the courts by Greenpeace, lose the case on the grounds that a proper consultative process has not taken place, and then complain that the Church of

England had no right to take the democratic decisions that it did. It would appear Mr Gummer is a little confused between romantics and semantics.

We had a cracking ethics lecture today. The subject was money. We discussed usury, puffed about how much was enough. The lecturer was eloquently goading us into revolution much of the time. The dilemma towards the end of the session was revolution from within, in other words taking a Christian stance within your employed capacity, or revolution from scratch. Both have their good points but as it was said, perhaps such things as 'Christian businesses' need starting otherwise more Christians will simply be fired or resign on issues of conscience. Apparently when Charles Wesley started his ministry he earned £30 a year, he lived on £27 and gave the remaining three pounds away. By the end of his life he was earning £300 a year, living on £27 and giving the rest away. It's plain that what is enough for some is not enough for others. I'm becoming increasingly convinced that Christianity rests on human choice; we make hundreds of decisions every day. Faith in Christ means perhaps that the consequences of those decisions are more carefully scrutinized and at best they are taken in the presence of the Holy Spirit.

Decisions driven by the desires of humanity in the absence of God have taken us to the very brink of disaster. It is not surprising that the church, as judged from a Western capitalist perspective, is viewed as irrelevant and ineffectual. Both its irrelevance and ineffectiveness actually serve the greed that is decimating our world. It is impossible within that reality for the church to be seen as anything else. The mistakes we have made largely revolve around having been entrapped by the capitalist mentality; our credible desire to serve those living and working within that system has been overrun by the system itself. At the very least the church, given the words of Christ and the action of the Holy Spirit, ought to be a reference point for a credible counter-culture. Christianity will remain impotent as long as we are involved in the very fabric of the greed machine. Our choices as Christians are ultimately made for us by the whims of the money markets and the smiles of the property speculators, having placed our trust in them we deserved no less than a bloody nose.

We all drove up to the Fens on Sunday to have a look at the parish. The sun decided to shine. We met the church-wardens who asked me whether I liked sport. The chairman of the school governors immediately dived in with an impassioned plea for me to coach the football team. It's definitely closer to the mark. We had a very bohemian lunch with the vicar, his twin brother, his wife, the vicar's sister, her husband and his 86-year-old mother. I wasn't grilled on the ordination of women, lampooned for going to an Evangelical college. My wife wasn't cornered by anyone and threatened with the flower rota, cleaning the brass and running a Bible study group. It felt like home. I hope it will be. There's nowhere to hide in the Fens, it's a landscape that I would imagine affects people deeply.

A suspicion of spring seems to have inspired the clouds to indulge in the madness of the season's courtship rituals. The chaffinches and blackbirds look varnished and the starlings sparkle in the sunshine flashes. The wind blowing the shrill squabbling of the sparrows and the distant sirens together. I found the beginnings of a nest after lunch stitched precariously into a leafless hedge. I think it was a song thrush. Unlike blackbirds they line the inside of their nests with mud, consequently they are a little deeper; anyway I'll watch from a distance. We've been allowed to use the garden opposite, it's more of a square really. I creep in after lunch every day. There are two main areas of grass, the top area is scattered with purple crocuses. They've planted it beautifully. There are very few straight lines. The huge poplar in the middle is surrounded by an irregular circle of daffodils and there are large clusters of snowdrops peeking through the cropped grass, brilliant in the cold sunshine.

I owe Gordon a beer. We got the job. The letter came through yesterday as well as a heap of forms and two very boring booklets from the Church Commissioners, one on stipends and the other on expenses. Essentially clergy get expenses for stationery, transport, telephone, entertaining. Some dioceses allow a little bit for robes and everyone is paid moving expenses, which I must say is very generous and which in our case won't be cheap. It's a horrifying thought; in four months' time I'll be expected to know the Bible inside out, every word of every hymn, every fine point surrounding every quivering edge of doctrine, and the quirks of ecclesiastical history that have led us into the present bunfight.

Yesterday we set off with doctrine, 'the God of Creation'. We then lost 3–1 at football. I then cooked curry for eight. Poacher started on white wine and graduated to rosé. He followed that with two different types of red wine and washed the whole lot down with prawn crackers and half a pint of port. I found him this morning lying in our study. First he told me that he'd only been a little bit sick, then he said his wife had taken the piss out of him all morning and then he asked for a glass of water. He has been under a lot of pressure; the college is suffering, the regime is overheating. This morning we coughed through the Psalms and twenty-three out of sixty-five of us spluttered through the intercessions. One person has left early; another hasn't slept for two nights, his mind shredded into shouting pieces of remembered verses and sermon crescendos.

I saw the advertisement for 'The Rector's Wife' which is being serialized on television. It features the actress with the wedding ring hovering halo fashion over her head. The line reads, 'the rector's wife can't wear it any more'. I have a feeling that over the next two days it will be mysteriously transformed into either 'The rector's wife fronts won't wear any more' or 'the rector won't wear it any more'.

The politics of nominations is hotting up. There's been a steady stream of closet megalomaniacs dropping in and out of the study to discuss the demands of being archdeacon. All the others are up for grabs as well; food friar, social secretary, so the jockeying of sorts will carry on unabated until lunchtime today when nominations for archdeacon close.

I spent the weekend in the Black Mountains. There was snow up on the tops and a wild wind that fired horizontal hail into our faces. The noise was so great it was impossible to hear someone yelling at full force two feet away from you. As the wind abated the mist came down. The only other people we saw in the morning were a small group from the Artillery Regiment who were carrying packs half the size of their bodies. They appeared out of the mist and then disappeared back into it again leaving flashes of their serious smiles.

I got back late last night to find my wife raging about 'The Rector's Wife' again. Apparently there had been a call in on Radio Four featuring a host of rectors' wives, all saying that Joanne Trollope's portrayal of a family who never stop talking about money and are dominated by the dangerous preconceptions of comfortable churchgoers was a far cry from fiction. It's no good saying money doesn't matter then paying someone so little that their every move is effectively dominated by it. It's counter-productive.

Money does matter, it matters very much. The church seems to have missed the point here. In the absence of choice and spending power to tout the view that money doesn't matter comes across as an ethereal edict.

If we were to support the idea of Christian communities/ communes where in effect we all worked for each other that would be one thing. But we don't; we are tangled up in the system, we are an institution governed by money. I get very depressed when I hear that most of the vicarages which were built in the Fifties and Sixties are all falling apart because they were built on the cheap. We cannot live this life without shelter, food and clothes. These are not possessions, they are necessities; they become possessions when they possess us. However, if we are forced to build, it is our Christian duty to build with sustainable, sensitive and locally bought materials and also to design something that will not only last but also enhance the local community. Surely we are to build for the glory of God not, as is so often the case, for the expedience of humanity, and that principle should be applied to cathedrals as well as a curate's flat. The Shakers in America adopted this principle and produced furniture and utensils that were not only beautifully and lovingly made but more importantly are still in use today. The natural resources we have been given by God, God's creation, are precious in the extreme and we should not sanction their wholesale abuse under the misguided principle of their material worthlessness and a practical utilitarian attitude that usually destroys practically everything for its own sake.

I have read several books recently that attempt to wriggle out of the word 'dominion' in Genesis, out of guilt for our clearly horrendous mistakes regarding the natural world and the sanctioned rape of its dignity, diversity and natural wealth. It is impossible for humanity to give up its 'dominion' over the world and it is pure fancy to pretend that the writer of Genesis didn't actually mean dominion.

It isn't our dominion that in itself is murdering this world. It is our application of that dominion. As long as we view a piece of land as having no intrinsic value other than to serve humanity, then we deny that land existence for its own sake. We effectively take God out of it and put humanity in. If we see a cow as a milking machine, we will labour under the lie that it is no more than that and again worthless for its own sake. If we poison the land with pesticides and nitrates then should we really be surprised if it poisons us? We not only create lifeless deserts but we destroy the soil and the very destroyers of the crops naturally mutate into forms beyond the reach of the original poisons. More terrifying is that we are in danger of arriving at a situation, if we are not already in it, where the world's population is dependant on fertilizers and pesticides. This self-created addiction will reap a dreadful environmental, moral and human harvest.

Yes, we are instructed to subdue the land. However, this has traditionally been achieved through violence. Most modern farm machinery resembles weapons of war through which we subject the environment to a reign of terror. We must learn that we can only enrich our natural world if we love it, as Christ showed us how to love. If we love the land and do what is best for it rather than what is best for us; if we love our cattle and our other livestock, then we will not fill them full of poisons to satisfy our gluttony and our greed. We will treat them with dignity. We need to inspire a relationship of respect and love with the natural world. Only then will we stop destroying it, we should take nothing for granted, it is wondrous in itself.

April 1994

The Arch-Evangelical was polish personified, neat hair, clean trousers, every bristle ruthlessly removed from his shining chin. His opponent, bespectacled, his brown loose-cut trousers hiding his quivering knees. It was all very polite. The motion for the debate was designed to furnish us all with an explanation of 'Reform'. 'Reform' represents the interests of the conservative wing of the Conservative Evangelicals. This college supports one paid-up member although there are clearly some lukewarm sympathizers. The result was a foregone conclusion. The Arch-Evangelical was destined to lose; it wasn't a question of by how much, it was more a question of how and what. He performed brilliantly, peeling delicate intellectual strips off the cash-guzzling ecclesiastical central bodies before verbally burning them in front of us. By his own admission the Church of England was the best boat to fish from. However, he was finally backed up the gangplank by one of our members who threatened him with the notion that reform was essentially about doctrinal purity and their claim to have it.

The general consensus afterwards was that these groups have cropped up throughout history on a regular basis. I don't think we should soothe our nerves with that notion. The last such major revival added not inconsiderable momentum to the onslaught of the English Civil War, closed all the theatres and arguably provided the stern moral tincture that causes numerous liberal hangovers to this day.

My main gripe is that the whole context of Reform's posturing is based on the literalism of the Bible. As our learned friend pointed out, it's predominantly Pharisaic. It gets its kicks out of its minority mentality and the dull assurance of its own salvation. I very much support the fact that these Conservative Evangelicals have formed their own club, purely because it's impossible to lance a boil you cannot see. But they are presenting themselves very professionally. Their logo is well thought out and there isn't a tulip or a sunset in sight so on that front I applaud them.

We actually won a football match having lost the last one 18–0. This came as more of a shock than anything else. But to the great relief of the Methodist goalkeeper and the beleaguered defensive line we've been relegated to Division Three. Four essays to go.

There is something curiously English about sunlight in churches. The shadows it spawns. Each church has its own sunlight refracted, distorted by the stained glass. The visions it produces hover between the sober and the sublime branding its presence on your memory, seizing your imagination in its fascinating contortions.

There were no lectures today; tomorrow we all have breakfast in our staircase groups, then a hall meeting for coded renditions on the State of the Nation. A communion meal in the evening followed by the vicars' disco—not to be missed.

Today was a quiet day; what that meant in practice was time to catch up on work. The work never stops. The good intentions of the calendar are obliterated by the practicalities of the timetable; theological reflection, something we're all encouraged to do, happens in the private spaces, not the scheduled ones; it's the nature of the beast.

The ex-archdeacon and I shared a beer. We came to the conclusion that ministry in the Church of England broadly falls into two categories, the vocational and the career-orientated. Neither of us were at all keen on the career model; however, it is unwise, I would suggest, to begin ministry not having loosely sorted out in your own mind which of the two you are to be committed to. Given the best of both worlds there would only be one, the vocational model; however, it is naive to assume the other does not exist and even more foolish to pretend it doesn't have a purpose, albeit its own.

They both involve suffering. I have come to the conclusion that the Christian embrace of suffering is probably the point that separates Christianity from society. Science, it would seem, to maintain its power, promises us all a pain-free existence. Its self-imposed purpose is to free us all from physical and emotional suffering, touting pills, perfume, plasters and all the promises of a miracle cure.

Christians, however, view suffering as part of the fabric of life, as unavoidable. We accept it as a vital part of our freedom, as an integral constituent of our emotional experiences, not as something to be calmed with Valium and 'Dallas' but more as the vehicle for the healing power of the Holy Spirit. Our hero Christ suffered the excesses of vested interest and abuse of power, he even believed at one point that God had deserted him. Suffering appals us but it is ultimately where we meet the loneliness, the strength, the resilience of humanity. There is within suffering the potential, it seems, to demonstrate the immense dignity and beauty of humanity. If we lose sight of that then we condemn ourselves to the eternal emptiness of another murder media headline. The pain of humanity becomes no more than merciless torture without Christ. Christianity is able to face suffering because of the reality of Christ's suffering, we are maybe less willing to smother it in Valium, to spend our way out of it, because we recognize perhaps its importance in confirming our humanity. It doesn't leave us less human, it makes us more so.

My fifteen-minute session with the doctrine lecturer stretched into an hour. It took the chill off a rather bald statement I'd rushed off in an essay. I was hanged for it at the time, deservedly so. This was the chat with the general to put me back on the straight and narrow. I'd allowed my passion to cloud my judgment. It's a mistake I make all the time. The end of term has raced by, my stint as social secretary is over, the vicars' disco was a low-key affair. In the absence of any sexual parade the dancing is mere role play, the posturing and prancing fulfilling no other function than to get off on the music, would-be vicars mouthing the lyrics of songs steeped in acid and back-seat sex appeared as surreal as a hardened heavy metal band speaking in tongues. Christianity has clearly lost the initiative to define who we are. That's something largely dictated by the media, as is what constitutes fun, what we all enjoy. No one identifies with the trainspotter because we've all been told what a plonker he is; we believe that at our peril. It's no good pretending to be groovy because you'll simply end up acting someone else's version of it. Trying to be groovy is even worse. Far better to be a trainspotter and be done with it. We will never be taken seriously by the media as it currently stands because the media is driven by the economic realities of the business community. So what's cool is what sells, or even better what would sell if we could afford it. As long as we believe that an airline is about booze, wide seats and pretty girls, then the reality is that we do not have a choice. If we believe that luxury is a big house, a yacht and a pink Rolls Royce then we are as helpless as all the other victims of that poisonous charade.

Christian culture in the West is lifeless because we are essentially pretending we're not really dancing to the music of the machine, we're playing at it; we're not doing it properly because we can't. We dance and sing beautifully to a different music. It's not always easy to hear it above the massed hum of money changing hands. Surely Christ presents all of us with his imagination. He speaks to our imagination of a world at peace, of justice for creation; that is where we meet him.

The Holy Spirit speaks to us on all levels but if we are only operating with our heads and our hearts, if we have surrendered our imaginations to the deadly disco of the western world then we will be imprisoned in the practical and captive to the sensational. If we cannot allow God to dream in us with all the peril that promise brings; if we fail to recognize the trinity within us of mind, body and spirit, then our response to Christ will be disabled by our timid expectations because we will stubbornly cling on to a vision and an imagination of our own making. We are in a sense suffering from creativity crisis as Christians. A crisis of the imagination.

The Charismatics came off very badly in the last episode of 'The Rector's Wife'. The new vicar, tambourine in tow, flashing semolina smiles, had the congregation wincing at every inflection of spiritual happiness. What my wife noticed was that the script wasn't interrupted constantly by the telephone once the rector's wife had actually moved out of the vicarage.

The phone didn't appear to have its bell tested much at Church House either. Three days in the communications department, however, was an interesting exercise. I can report the Church of England is not in decline. Congregations have, in fact, stabilized around 1.4 million. Like most figures these are no less subject to interpretation but this fact seemed to be generally accepted. However, there still seems to be little sense of direction and any sense of who is doing the driving. The problem seems to be the absence of a power base. The Church of England tends to have power bases whose *raison d'être* is to spend most of their time guarding that power. I saw the new logo. The brief was for something dynamic. Something that encapsulated movement. What has emerged is a plus sign surrounded by crushed tadpoles.

The radio course was a different kettle of fish altogether. There were four of us. A leading light in the Sea of Faith movement, a hospital chaplain and a Roman Catholic priest. We were ruthlessly instructed on the art of a thought for the day and then hung drawn and quartered *en masse* by a professional radio interviewer who reduced each one of us to spouting incoherent drivel simply to highlight the fact that we must 'prepare our sound bites' have them etched in our brain beforehand.

I was shown the debating chamber of General Synod: rooms full of paintings of past Reverends, and endless corridors of closed doors with black nameplates on them. The most memorable of these was the handyman plaque: someone had switched the H for an R. So it is human after all, as maybe he is. My overriding impression is that in the absence of control on any agreed policy the system is prone to maverick assaults and can do little but react rather than plan. Any clout that we have is also really undermined by the fact that as a body we expend vast amounts of energy catching up with the present rather than planning for a future. The future was something I sensed people did not have confidence in. It was a place of fear and foreboding rather than a land full of opportunity and promise. We are behaving as if we are besieged which I believe signifies that we have, in fact, bought into the secular value system rather than developed our own. There is a massive loss of confidence; you can see it in people's eyes. Yes, we can all become Evangelicals touting cast-iron biblical certainty, leaflets and videos on youth work and the perils of euthanasia, but I tend now to view Evangelicals as a response, a reaction almost, to the current crisis rather than a solution. I accept the fact that the Evangelical fortress as it's become is a far safer place to live in as a Christian in the current climate and even that some people are happy there.

I am not. It is a regimented Christianity that is primarily opposed to the world. The view from the fortress, like most fortresses, is hostile. It is no wonder that the sight of 'Evangelicals winning souls for Christ' looks so like a military campaign. I deplore the fact that the current economic system means that we have all declared war on creation, that we are all essentially at war with each other simply to survive on its terms. But I do not feel as Christians we should adopt the same tactics.

If God loves the world he loves it as it is and I am of the opinion he loves the sinner as much as the saint. I am not prepared to hate the world for what it is and then depend on it for my very survival, or adopt the luxury of passivism as I swallow food that has been procured through the ecological brutality and violence of fertilizers and pesticides.

If we truly loved each other, truly loved each other as Christ asked us to do then fortresses would not be necessary.

The Principal wants to reorder the Chapel. At the moment there are rows of carved pews which follow the wall, with an open space in the middle. He wants carpets, chairs and sympathetic lighting. I favour God's light bulb myself. As Christians we ought to be able to worship anywhere. If he doesn't like his Principal's pew he shouldn't sit in it, he doesn't have to. If our worship is hindered by carved wooden pews it's our own fault, not the pews'. The new Waterboys' album is magnificent.

We can see humanity's treatment of God meted out to us in every newspaper, news flash and tragic report. We arrogantly assume that this is human suffering, it is divine suffering ordained by humanity.

Part of me is dying, I can feel it. I'm having my all, my reassuring dependencies like cigarettes, sex, charm, ripped out by the roots. Consequently I am at war with myself. The battle rages while normality and even peace seem as hostile strangers.

The last term has started. We had the usual hall meeting. In fact it wasn't the usual hall meeting. There was a report from the mean streets of Manchester, a mission update from the Masai Mara and brief recollections of life on a Suffolk mission, the one I refused to go on. Finally, there were tales from a camp fire in eastern Europe where the ethics lecturer was trapped in the loo for half an hour. He claimed that was tantamount to experiencing solitary confinement in a Communist country. We then had some prayer. It was good to be back.

I've got one month left to write four essays and then I'm ordained six weeks later. The letters have started coming. We had a long one from the Diocesan Secretary's Secretary. We're allowed twenty tickets for the ordination at the Cathedral and there's what's called drinks back at the Bishop's place afterwards. The snag is only ten people are invited from each party, so what do you do with the remainder? I'm going up to see the boss on Friday to sort out days off, expectations, expenses and also to meet the Diocesan Surveyor who's going to come and give the house the once over.

The reality of being ordained is so close. I am not prepared at all, not mentally. I am definitely more helpless now than when I arrived. I am confident in less of my faith, and more in the feeling of faith, the experience of the presence of God. I am not convinced I am doing the driving—it feels like automatic pilot. I have no choice but to trust it. It's not an uncomfortable feeling, quite the opposite actually, it is a great sense of timelessness behind our conception of time.

Bart is really suffering. He spent all of last term working at a hospital for the mentally ill. The experience has taken its toll. All the old boundaries he had have been bombed out. I spoke to him briefly at lunch; he's not the type of man to explode his doubts but it was plain to see he was suffering.

It was actually warm today. I saw a peacock butterfly. It danced over the path. There's also a tawny owl whooping it up at college; it must have a nest nearby. I hope it doesn't find the mouse that runs to and fro in front of the kitchen window; it's exquisite. It has a sleek elegant coat and paper-thin ears.

On the subject of mousy-coloured hair, the Principal was in flying form this morning. We had a three-hour session on leadership where I don't think he actually breathed out ever apart from to parry a few challenges from the floor. It was essentially terrifying, the confrontations and, worse, the salutations. I've decided to keep my trap firmly shut for the first three months and just listen; that's the best thing I can do, listen to God and the Fens.

May 1994

I met Hardy Amis the fashion designer at a baptism; what an elegant man. His friend felt the church lacked leadership, colour, and flair. I'm becoming increasingly confused whether it can possess these things or whether it is possessed by them. Mr Amis said women should never have chocolate on their faces, only on their lips. My wife would agree. The vicar doing the baptism looked buggered. He had small kaleidoscope eyes. He also felt the church was low on characters and fuel. We ploughed through the baptism service, the format of which has obviously been agreed by some liturgical committee. I can see it now, everyone's got their halfpenny's worth in there.

I was standing behind my future godson, looking out at the congregation, watching their eyes as the vicar read the words off the sheet. They were lost after the second sentence; these fine and beautiful words had washed over them since childhood. They'd never been explained. No one after the service had the slightest idea of what it all meant, not really. But they loved it, every second. It actually required nothing of them other than their silence and it was the silence they craved, a huge silence filled with the God of their dreams. Untroubled by our days of doctrine and unencumbered with our shameful division.

God can be no more than our idea of God. That definitely does not make God an idea. Christ is not an idea, but I would suggest that our doctrine requires just as much faith as our faith. No one believed in the incarnation today, no one knew what it meant apart from the vicar and myself: does that make them worse Christians or better? And even if they had all been subject to baptism preparation classes, would that have made them any more Christian than the engine drivers, shepherds, and stockmen whose names fill the old baptism registers?

We need to earth Christianity through creation, through the Christ of creation. I feel he has a lot in common with the God of the empty spaces.

The interest-free car loan has had its day. The Church Commissioners will now charge 5 per cent on all cash borrowed by clergy to purchase a motor. This generation are going to somehow have to find the £500,000,000 that our forebears blew on the property market. 5 per cent is still very generous. However, most people got the news from the national press rather than the church press. Not a great way to do things really.

Yesterday belonged to South Africa. There was a feeling of near elation from all those who had visited the country and knew the townships. There was a great sense that a great evil had been defeated and that prayer had been answered. We had an evening service with a Township liturgy, it was bristling with rebellion through love; it was active, hopeful, and realistic. Fabulous. The future was a place of dreams; the dream of justice, integrity and equality for all races. The future dream is on the threshold of embracing reality. It cannot be sustained. I hope disappointment will not lead to disenchantment; racists sadly cannot be changed by the ballot box. But what a day.

We hit the pub afterwards for a quick half. Two pints later we had the sobering thought that hell might actually be full of people who never stop smiling and when confronted with a problem say 'I hear what you say', a place where everybody is incredibly nice to each other all the time. A place that exists on a surface of smiles and is no deeper than that; it is empty of anger, frustration, disagreement, happiness, it is empty of everything; it is the victory of non-existence, the victory of the advertising smile over reality.

We as Christians are supposed to believe in one God, but the reality is that we have a God each. There is nothing more obscene than Protestants killing Catholics and vice versa simply because it cries out loudly My God; it's *my* God: it isn't *our* God. It's the same with possessions, the very fact that I own possessions; that they are mine means that other people are forced to own theirs. We own things in isolation from each other. We perhaps need a society where we own less and borrow more.

The reality of our lives means that all we do, all we ever do, is borrow either from the past, the present, or currently steal from the future. Owning things is merely an intrusion. We can be given responsibility for land, animals, each other, but the moment we allow ourselves to believe we own things we are in deep, deep trouble.

Non-human creation reflects, acts very much as a mirror to, the mental state of humanity because it is that creation we essentially try to possess. It is a pointless exercise; we can never have it. We can only ever be responsible for it. There are those who say that God's command/gift of dominion is what has caused this ecological crisis. I disagree. Human beings have never behaved as if they have responsibility for this planet and the life it contains. We, the spoilt children, have taken what we wanted with no thought for anyone else let alone a creator God. It is only when we start to behave as if we have dominion, which was in itself a gift from God, over this planet that we will declare a state of peace between ourselves and the environment. We are at war with our environment, at war with each other.

We walked yesterday from Avebury to Stonehenge: 22 miles in 5 hours 40 minutes. It was one of those hot spring days. I've never approached Stonehenge on foot; it's always much smaller than I imagined. I used to stop there when I was a child before they cordoned it off and charged people to look at it, which is a bloody cheek anyway; it belongs to everybody, not English Heritage, or Wiltshire County Council, or whoever they are. I suppose it was bound to succumb to the owning disease; what a pity. Two more essays to go.

I don't think I've ever been in so much pain as I have experienced over the last three weeks. It was an absolute isolation where everything had a meaningless potential. I would wake up in the middle of the night utterly desolate. I'm hungover from it now, drained and shattered. It's easy as a Christian to put everything down to God, the way you pick up a biscuit and watch a film; it can all become very fatalistic. The people that indulge in this sort of voluntary surrender of one's character become liturgical androids and gospel robots. It actually works against the body of Christ in the end because everyone can only do one thing; there is no exchange of ideas because nobody has any. It kills our humanity by denying it. Christians always seem to be such imperfect people. We carry our wounds and scars around in a basket. This is good. We are not hiding behind perfection or society's idea of it. We are bold enough to be imperfect. It is a living hell having to pretend otherwise. I've seen it happen. Middle-class men seem to suffer from this 'copes disease'; they cope with having to pretend everything is all right when it isn't. They cope with a job they can't stand. They cope with wanting more but never being able to afford it. They cope with life. They end up believing the lies; they've learned to signal confidence, wherewithal, and to impress each other. It kills them inside, kills their humanity completely. I remember once tendering for some business and having this half-hour conversation about golf. The client and I exchanged putting tips and stories about how we'd handled Seve's divot or Woosenham's tee. We fixed a date for a round together. I've never played golf in my life; I've never been one for the criss-crossed lambswool jumpers or the cropped countryside and the tie rule in the clubhouse, no it's not for me, but he swallowed it, all that bullshit. That was a watershed really; he didn't blink once and more terrifyingly neither did I. I am changing and I hate it. I want my reliable cigarettes, I want my indulgent sexual fantasies, my dream of winning a million; they protect me from reality, allow me to maintain my desperate vanity. They are being ruthlessly squeezed dry and it is very painful. But most of my previous life was a defence against feeling; it was an exercise in self-gratification: it involved no one other than me. I was the individual in the society for individuals. It was great; no, it really was, pain-free—the whole point of life was to avoid pain—but so destructive. Life stopped at the end of my nose. Nothing I did had any consequence beyond the next thought of the next hedonistic action. Christian life at its best is truly corporate, it's interdependent. This is why it is failing, because it is not competitive, not at its best. It has no need for competition because Christians will want the best for the other person. You come across the odd megalomaniac vicar or churchwarden but megalomaniac churchwardens at least are the exception rather than the rule. Seeing yourself for what you are is desperately painful; I can only stand a bit at a time.

I've had flu for a couple of days, miserable, along with the glorious rain. I started on the books at eight this morning: it's half past seven now. I haven't been to college, Poacher popped over this afternoon extolling the virtues of red wine and summer; he's finished all his essays, he doesn't have to do as many but that still didn't stop him looking immensely pleased with himself. So he should be, he's got six weeks of sound sleep left in his life, then baby number one arrives on this planet and he thinks he's losing his hair as it is.

Summer is here, the huge copper beech outside my window started off pink last week and has gradually become a rich luminous port colour worshipping the wind with every gust and flurry. My wife is working so my contact with the rhythms of theological training tend to become sporadic at best. I went in there today though. The incumbents' day has come round again. Poacher was being shadowed by an Anglo-Catholic from the West Country, sporting some serious Victorian sideboards; he was wearing regulation black, everything. He had a firm handshake and spiky eyes. The others looked, as usual, as if they'd walked off a jumble-sale catwalk apart from one Evangelical who was wearing a tie and smart suit jacket. I was introduced to him. I could see his smiling curate-to-be steering him round anyone who was likely to say he grew organic radishes. I've one essay left to do. The doctrine lecturer gave my last internal piece of work back and there in bold letters on the top was the magic word 'distinction'.

I've hit the wall, the pain is intense. A Jehovah's Witness rang me this morning trying to convince me that God and Christ provide a never-ending paradise of happiness. Christianity is immensely painful; it's the pain of giving up oneself, of seeing that a life spent seeking self-gratification is done so at the expense of everything and everybody else; for an utterly selfish individual like me that is a bitter pill to take. I have to go through this dreadful isolation, this overpowering melancholy. Creation gives; the copper beech gives of itself to me; the zebras, polecats, pigeons, make no charge; there's a given life which will ultimately feed another's needs; the lions cannot escape the vultures at the end. We need as human beings to give of ourselves to creation. I've come to the conclusion this stewardship model is nonsense; it merely separates creation from us, separates God from us; perpetuates the myth that we can live without charge. One more essay to go.

Well, it's finished. They're sitting next to me on the table, neatly enclosed in shining plastic; they're due in tomorrow at twelve o'clock. I finally realized this morning that nowhere in all of this training has anyone actually said that they really enjoy being a vicar. It's all been dour and serious, overflowing with problems and pointless meetings with frightened people.

The last doctrine lecture lived up to its usual billing; we looked at the resurrection of the body. The Evangelical faction suggested wryly that when we all go to heaven (tad presumptuous really) we'll be given a catalogue to choose a new heavenly body. The arch-Evangelical said he really fancied a forty-eight-inch chest. When it was pointed out to him that people didn't marry in heaven he tried back-tracking and insisting that it was *his* chest he was talking about, but by then he'd gone the colour of a red pepper and was obviously in no fit state to refute anything. Someone had actually defaced his picture hanging up with the rest of us on a notice board. They've added a small but nevertheless poignantly positioned black Hitler moustache.

I'm not really looking forward to being ordained, it's all rather final. People keep telling me the Fens has the highest rates of suicide, incest and divorce in the country. I can see why, looking over the flat land into the endless distance. It has a beauty, a very harsh beauty, but it is an island far away from pretty England. We're going up there on Thursday to meet the Assistant Diocesan Surveyor; he's calling to see what needs doing to the house. We're very lucky it's a big house: most curate's houses are particularly small and poky. I might go fishing on Monday.

There's always one moment that is spring, the other moments merely draw you to it or take you from it. How easy it would be to gaze like a junkie into the rich green, to have it all in that moment. The terrifying thing about being a vicar is that it is all so ruthlessly sensible, ruthlessly sober on the outside. The job is lousy; the perks are what I'm doing it for, to be swallowed by the distance, to have different terms of reference from those dictated by cornflakes and cars. The pain of every crushing Jesus that loves me, holds our dancing hearts. The Church of England is the vehicle, that's all, rusty, yes; worn out, yes: in need of a service, most definitely. I'm ordained in six weeks' time.

I drove up to the new house today to meet the Assistant Diocesan Surveyor. We dealt with the damp and the garden and the kitchen window. I will have to talk to the Archdeacon about the pink-tiled shower that appears as if it's been designed by the same people that build communist tower blocks and installed on a Friday afternoon by party officials with an axe to grind.

The short-course season is upon us once again; this week is Evangelism with Michael Green. How to hook the young, hold the old and harangue everyone else into the arms of Christ. He is clearly supremely gifted, the stuff Evangelists are made of. He doesn't so much talk as perform. He dances with Christ. We were the orchestra. I'm sure all his audiences are. He doesn't believe in ordained ministry. I'm not sure I do any more either. We isolated a tent full of reasons as to why people don't want to come to church. It ultimately came down to the fact, not that anybody said so, that God was not actually in church: he was not in the reasons why people failed to be inspired; he was not part of this antiquated, ritualized, sacred mediocrity. We were more likely to find him in a house church, preferably a New Testament model, bristling with tongues, shaking with prophecy, singing *Songs of Fellowship and Praise* at full volume from an overhead projector. Is this the new wine or the old wine in a new glass?

Do we mix the two together, fuse the past and the present: is that where we'll find the future? No. Christianity will continue to be an ineffectual club as long as we settle as Christians for this vision of the church and no more. All of this Evangelism was self-serving, creating more Christians in its own image of Christianity. Has the Charismatic movement really revitalized society? Or has it merely converted Christians to Charismatics? New Testament Christianity changed the world, that's irrefutable, we are living that legacy; to do it all over again in exactly the same way is senseless. The devil changes his clothes as the needs suit; you cannot fight computer pornography with an abacus. Michael Green did not pull his punches this evening; he accused us of being cowards closeted in theological cotton wool. He's right, but we're encouraged to be cowards; the system teaches compliance. He stood there shouting at us about the dangers of cynicism in the church and the dreadful legacy of respectability, here was at last some sense. But our great training system can only pass the respectable, it has become a respectable ghetto. Its response to its own dismal failure has been to close yet more theological colleges. There is no getting away from the fact that since the conception of formalized theological education church attendance has declined.

I was charged at by a swan yesterday. It ran across the water, its neck aimed at me, feet banging the surface. It stopped about two feet short of my boots, pulled up its wings and hissed. I didn't realize there was a nest round the river bend. This morning I went to the Franciscans' church. All the way through the prayers there was the sound of children laughing; it completely changed the meaning. We pray all the time for those areas of the world that are tearing themselves apart with war and famine. Our own conflicts rage inside us. We pray for God's grace, God's love. What is that in reality? What does it look like, feel like? It wasn't at all strange to hear the little girl laughing over the blood of Rwanda and the murderous monotony of Northern Ireland. We have made a severe God: see the dolphins, the seals in the waves, the singing thrushes, the selfless salmon: do they speak in hushed tones? Is the warm breeze of the desert eternally serious? The rain in summer melancholy? Christ allows us to bear our separation from it, our separateness from God. He speaks to that pain in us, recognizes our loneliness, but I'm sure he laughed; please God he must have laughed. If survival is so deadly serious then it can be no more than mere survival.

I have an oral exam tomorrow or the day after, then a course on death and dying, a full-day session on the parables of Christ, then that is it.

The swifts are back, dogfighting high above the roofs. The oral exam was an unmitigated disaster. I was chopped into little pieces and then minced. They had a point. I must have said the prayer concerned three times a week for the last two years. They merely proved I had the brain of a parrot and the verbal inconsistency to match. It wasn't a good morning. I sneaked into college twenty minutes late intent on creeping into Chapel upstairs and unseen. As I rounded the corner I nearly walked into two bishops and just as I was on my final approach the Principal appeared leaving the Chapel, the service had ended; it was a fair cop.

This morning we had what was termed as a 'resources morning' when divine salesmen from long established Christian organizations turn up and try to get us all to sign up to support missions in Angola, organize our time better, treat children as people and ungrind the organ. It was dull, predictable. We're all battle worn now; we did try our best to seem interested to lull the nervous speakers into confidence but we're all tired. We need some space. I'm off to walk around the Western Highlands, courtesy of some very generous friends.

June 1994

Three days of sheer joy, mountains, what mountains, huge, serious, dangerous, bleak and bloody. They were not to be trifled with. On the last day we decided to cut through an utterly empty expanse. It was meant to be a short hop, eight miles or so, but we made a mistake. We walked fourteen, the middle bit was through a moss-encrusted boulder field that cut your fingers and trapped your ankles. Occasionally the utter silence was punctured by the piccolo call of a worried oystercatcher, but they were singing to a desert. Humanity had not decided out of some well-meaning ecological philanthropy to leave this landscape to the weather. No, this was unconquered territory, nature had won. You could sense the blood that beauty spills in the fight for recognition and survival; this was a relentless place.

I was walking on my own and a lark flew up from the stunted black heather. She feigned injury to distract my eyes, falling over her wings, pretending to be clumsy. Hidden under the heather closeted in evenly wrapped golden strands of dried grass was a tiny nest holding two new pink chicks. In among the freezing flurries that slice through the moaning boulders was a space for that life. We mustn't think of it as hard, we must see it as perfect. It could be nowhere else, could be perfect nowhere else.

I came back to the death and dying course. We spent this morning mulling over the undercurrents of a funeral and the death of children and allowing children to express their own grief.

This afternoon it was our turn to visit the crematorium for a guided tour. It was a hot day. The building was everyone's idea of what a crematorium should be. Death made boring, death made bland. It was functional. There were no frills. Our guide was a small man. He took us into Chapel and showed us what buttons to press. We then filed in through a discreet door into a hot room. The ovens were on. The single ovens were on this side, on the other side of the building there were some newer double ovens. We peered in through the peep holes and saw the glowing leg bones, hip joints and pelvis of somebody who had been walking around not too long ago. Thin bodies take longer to burn than fat ones. The gas and air mixture which gets the whole process going is crucial with a fat body. The EEC are very tight on crematorium emissions and fat people tend to burn 'too well'. There was quite a big bloke in the third oven. Our guide opened up the front. Most of the flesh had burned off, it was impossible to see the heads of the bodies, everything was done from the feet end. Once the bodies had burnt what was left was collected in a chute. What comes out of the oven is not ashes, it is essentially pieces of bone. It's all very discernible, a hip joint here, a bit of skull there. It's not at all macabre. These pieces of bone are then put in a large tumble dryer which has half a dozen or so steel balls inside to grind down the bone to ash. The caskets which the ash goes into are far heavier than I though they would be. Our guide said he would most definitely be cremated which gave us the confidence of *le patron mange ici*. Nevertheless my wife and I had a light supper and skirted round the delights of tomorrow's excursion to the funeral parlour.

The funeral parlour was memorable. He gave us the usual introduction. He was a neat middle-aged man, softly spoken, close-cropped hair and kind eyes. He told us that coffins were made out of chipboard these days, the veneers were different; real cherry wood, oak and ash were a thing of the past. The brass handles were plastic. He said he wouldn't and didn't charge for children's funerals; very few undertakers do. The babies' coffins were stacked right up at the back. There were also some children's coffins. They were about half the size of adult ones. Undertakers do everything, the cars, the flowers, the paperwork. I didn't realize you simply turned up and wrote the cheque, which is currently just over a thousand pounds. They all were also on call 24 hours a day 365 days of the year.

There are some bastards out there who hoax-call undertakers. They'll turn up at a house where no one has died. It's obviously meant as a warning; the undertakers roll up with your name as the body in question; not a very pleasant thing to do.

The bloke lying in the Chapel of rest was eighty-two. He'd been dead for several days. At the request of the family he hadn't been embalmed. His eyes were a little sunken and the ends of his fingers almost purple. He'd had a post mortem so the funeral gown covered the scar on his neck. He was cold to touch, rather like uncooked chicken.

There were three bodies in the fridge, an elderly woman and an elderly man in his pyjamas who both were covered over, their heads were by the door. We looked at their faces; the elderly woman had been embalmed. The skin on her face was much firmer. The other body was in a closed coffin. I think the undertaker must have been relaxed, I'm not sure that the rest of us were. I was at the front. He simply lifted the lid off the coffin whilst he was talking. Inside was the body of a 47-year-old woman; she must have been beautiful. She'd died in hospital; the tops of her hands were white where the doctors had threaded the drip into her veins. She looked utterly and totally exhausted. She'd been dressed in a blue dress and had a sprig of freesias placed in her clasped hands. Her face was the colour of sand. I wasn't really ready for the lid coming off; it's something I won't forget. Her body looked broken by the disease she had been suffering from. I don't know what it was.

I'm not sure whether looking at dead bodies can really be described as disturbing. It's more humbling. There is definitely nobody there, in them; they've gone. You can't even guess at the characters, not really. They are shells, husks, they can tell no tales. They can do nothing except remind us that it will be our turn one day at a time that is rarely of our own choosing. They can dispel our more ludicrous notions that we govern and have ultimate control even for one second and leave us grappling with the reality of our own crematorium ashes.

The lady this morning had worked in a hospice for the dying. She told us death was not in 95 per cent of cases painful. Most of us will simply drift into unconsciousness. There are more unpleasant ways to die but mercifully they are few and far between. She did tell us one story of a young mother who advertised for and interviewed nannies to look after her children once she had died. We will all of us, given time to die, face the guilt of broken relationships and our own selfishness. We all of us regard our deaths as perhaps untimely; there is always more to do. A vicar's job is quite simply to try and explain that death is a gateway rather than a hole in the ground. We're allowed to talk about heaven, hell, God, Jesus, judgment. I would say that what we can do is to prepare people for meeting Christ so that they can recognize him, recognize him in them and them in him. That their lives can be viewed in the light of love, rather than the pain of dissatisfaction, emptiness and alienation.

It was another open day yesterday; they all looked like good Christians, neat, tidy, inoffensive, unexciting, uninspiring. Are these prerequisites to being chosen by God? I doubt it. The people who will be living in this house came and looked round. I think they liked it. It is a beautiful house, it has a timeless light about it and the view of the copper beech as the wind laps at her leaves is captivating. Next week is my last week, term ends for me on Friday morning.

Today some eminent doctor sat on a chair he must cart around the country with him and told us all about Christ in the context of his own contemporary culture. It was fascinating: we delved into the table manners of ancient Palestine; the memory banks of a culture which, according to our eminent professor recognized and identified itself through an utterly precise oral tradition. What we see as haphazard in the New Testament is apparently not so. There are ordered stanzas influenced by the early fathers of the Old Testament. Apparently we mustn't view the New Testament as unreliable because of its dependence on oral traditions, much of middle Eastern culture is dependent to this day on oral traditions.

After two years here he appeared as another academic minstrel, plucking at the strings of intellect. They each have their own tunes they would like us to learn. Books they would like us to buy. Very few of them have actively done anything other than think. Their theories litter our consciousness: their words polluting the silence, screaming to be heard in the ceaseless struggle to be courted and quoted. Christ did not only say, he did. There was action. He scared the living shit out of the complacent, the self-righteous, the arrogant, the apathetic, all those too lazy to go the extra mile, that's all of us now. To dress Christianity in nice inoffensive wrapping paper is offensive in itself. The professor today was brittle. He shouted at us and refused to answer our questions; he was almost rude. Maybe that was his calling card. It made no difference; he was showing us nothing and telling us little that we couldn't work out for ourselves.

Well, it's done. There was a sting in the tail though. I failed my oral examination. It would have been the crowning farce to have passed it. I can't say I'm that fussed. It was a lousy course. I passed the essays. There were three credits all for stuff I threw together in a hurry. I sweated blood on the doctrine and only passed that, so it's all still rather hit and miss. I'm not in control of this academic virus inflicted on us. I have a feeling the examiners want to be taken by the hand and not tested too vigorously. Anything that wavers too far from the norm and requires effort and is a diversion from the tried and tested marking procedure is red-penned. I'm not sure I'm that enamoured with academic discipline; it is ultimately self-serving and rewards no one other than the academic. This defining of intelligence is really a form of dictatorship because it recognizes nothing else other than its own code as being of any worth. It's perhaps what you learn in the shadows, in the space between right and wrong, that's interesting.

Why the church has to entertain grandiose notions of book culture when the majority of the country is divorced in terms of direct cultural input from the railway tracks of academic theology is beyond me. Theological college sets us apart and we will, I believe, spend the rest of our lives as vicars mourning the separation. Theological college really reflects the crisis that besieges the Church of England. The function of the Church of England, or if you like Christianity in the West, is quite different from its purpose. The Church of England is a church whose purpose has been sterilized by its function, our function has become our purpose. We are all of us being trained for a model of ministry that quite simply is failing not only the church but more importantly those who do not attend. The vicar as he/she is largely perceived is a cultural relic. Ray Illingworth, who has unceremoniously dumped the test side's chaplain, says he wants players who don't need a shoulder to cry on. Our words, fine words, are little substitute for action. Mr Illingworth quite rightly, in my opinion, takes a knife to Cliff Richard Christianity because in terms of original content, much like most of Mr Richard's music, it offers a low return. Mr Illingworth's definition of what it is to be a man, however, is deeply worrying.

The review seemed quieter than normal and the leavers' dinner had the usual flying table mat festivities. It's not as bad as I thought it would be to be leaving. I was dreading it really. Bart has one more year to do. He's still undecided about his future. I think he passed this year's crop of essays with distinction, but his work experience has really beached his faith or rather faith as it was; he has too many questions that have no answers. Those of us who are leaving were given a certificate saying that we had been diligent, trustworthy and so on. However, it really read more as if we'd successfully completed a weekend course.

All institutions end up by sucking you in; the minute details of people's lives and especially the cracks that appear in those that run them take on fascinating proportions. It happens in every industry and it happens with depressing monotony in the church. It has been, though, an immense privilege. I have been prayed for, fed, my mind watered, all in the name of the Church of England, the pennies to pay my fees coming from those that cannot afford to part with them. I can honestly say it has changed me; the medicine has worked. God has become a much bigger reality than I ever believed possible, the Holy Spirit a far more intimate companion than my sanity would previously have dared entertain. Christ is an immense and divine marker in human history whose love shines through the mere shadows of our lives. In Christ is the hope of humanity; without him, his presence, we are no more than parasites feeding off the stars. Life can be no more than a brutal departure from the drudgery of physical survival and the purity of space.

My relationship with my wife has deepened tremendously. This change has had its bloody battles. It is not easy to accept some of the more blatant double standards of Christians who proffer love to those within the club and appear to make little or no effort at all with anyone who does not share their own Christian beliefs. It is impossible to feel prepared, ready. There is too much happening at once. We have to move house in a week. I then must go on retreat with the ordaining Bishop for four days. The overriding impression is that something has definitely happened to you, but you cannot quite put your finger on what it is.

It's been a warm two days, a breeze has taken the edge of luxury out of the sunshine but it was there nevertheless, the sky endlessly blue. I went back to college, they're doing a course on Herod; clusters of ordinands sitting on the lawn were thumbing pages of the Bible. We're taught to teach, not to do. This teaching model has infected all the churchmen/women of this century—Vicars have studies lined with books. The result is a ministry of words. Our platitudes eked out from the pulpit are as meaningless as they are all potentially hypocritical. We follow a man who walked the desert from our armchairs, as a church we are clearly aligned with the Establishment and we expend most of our energy ingratiating ourselves towards it. In attempting to be accommodating Christianity has in the West essentially been accommodated by a political establishment that needs a tame religion to hide its sins behind and pose for pictures, usually dressed in black mourning, with the charlatans that call themselves our public servants.

I'm quite sure that life beyond theological college is a deal more dirty, but we leave it brandishing books in the face of hypodermic syringes, staggering deceit and the clean corporate cuffs sporting perfect fingernails that are tearing this planet to shreds. Most of us, it must be said, are not schooled beyond the boundaries of doctrinal politics and I would severely question the majority of ordinands who harbour ambition for high ecclesiastical office. Careerism is probably the single factor that has, over generations, sucked most integrity and vitality out of the church, because it demands conformity. I would argue passionately that we are called to serve God, not to serve ourselves. It is hardly surprising that with the emphasis placed on academics, faith itself has become academic. The church's heartland is in the mind. With the rise of the Evangelicals this malaise can only deepen. Our faith needs to infect our hearts, we must feel it; we will sing it much better than if we think it.

We move house in a few days' time; most of the others have gone. There is a great sense really of 'awaiting your fate'. Life is much more fragile than we ever dare believe. It would take no more than a minute to destroy everything we have built around ourselves. Our marriages, our jobs, these are delicate things that exist only because we happen to believe in them at the time. The person that came to theological college is very different from the one that is leaving. The boy cannot know the man and the old man cannot know the young man. We are marooned in the present as we are. Our dreams have us believe we can escape; we cannot, not yet.

I'm not very good with goodbyes, merely because I don't believe in them. I've decided to write to the people I purposely didn't say goodbye to. There was little camaraderie at theological college; a few of us may keep in touch with each other but it's a big 'may'. I suppose I found it a lonely experience; there was always so much to do, friendships need quality time, there was little of that; everything was done in a hurry, squeezed into spaces, in between spaces. We fought private wars; there wasn't enough time to die for each other. I don't actually believe that as a process it has any idea of what it wants to achieve. There are all these bits tacked on which don't seem to fit into a grand scheme of anything. If one was to follow the letter of theological living and pass everything with distinction, I don't actually feel it would make that much difference to the Church of England. Poacher has left for the delights of his Anglo-Catholic parish in Exeter. His wife is expecting a baby today, it's late. Imagine you don't even know where the light switch is let alone where you put the saucepans, and you're wandering around with a newborn baby trying to encourage it to close its eyes at four in the morning. Marvellous.

It's been very sunny, hot and slow, lovely. The packers are in with us today taping everything into boxes. The blackbird has laid a third clutch of eggs in the ivy. The young ones from the previous clutches keep coming into the house. They peck at the crumbs on the kitchen floor or they are caught in the glass kaleidoscope of the sitting room hurling themselves at the windows and shitting everywhere. I went into college this morning to hand back the keys for my room and for the dining room and the rest of it. It was all very quiet, awaiting the onslaught of the language students who apparently laugh a great deal, sunbathe on the grass and have affairs. The idea of celibacy before marriage is meaningless if it is enforced by a jealous god; it is a beautiful idea but it is made beautiful by personal decisions rather than authoritarian edict. If young people do not grasp the 'idea' we must not blame them or accuse them of lust and abandon. It is the failure of the church to interest them in the idea of celibacy, the idea that sex without love robs people of their dignity, they become meat and no more. We have failed to explain that sex is sensational which is why it is so precious.

Theological college is a battleground. We fight over God, over what God is. This wanting God for ourselves, wanting the God of our terms, has drained Christianity of colour. In our attempts to love a God we can all recognize we have created a God that conforms to what we want him/her to be. The church has made the mistake of owning God; it is a travesty that we shall suffer for many years to come. Until we can get back to God owning us we are doomed to suffer the tacit support of the power and people that we mistakenly believe we need to exist. What most people in fact want is a God confined to the church, a God cast in doctrinal and dogmatic cement and suffocated by liturgical tradition, a God unmoved by our casual greed, and Christians they can laugh at.

Up in the Flatlands

I have a different view. There are three chimneys and four aerials but behind them the sky goes on forever. The first person I saw when I opened the door was the Principal, he was lying on the floor his teeth grinning up at me from the cover of some Church Pastoral Aid magazine. We've been here for five days. We've unpacked 180 boxes. The house was designed by the Church Commissioners; it reeks of red tape and has an air of cut corners. If you sat down for too long on the carpets in a pair of synthetic trousers you'd generate enough electricity to kill yourself. The Diocese have been very diligent and painted the hall and the landing white and there was a bloke round today to mend the taps who told me that 80 per cent of the clergy he speaks to are 'tossers'. My daughter has asked to go home about five times now. She's been pretty tearful and unable to sleep. I've told her it's my fault and that she must blame me, which I hope she will. She seemed a bit more settled today, tearing round and round the house on her bike.

It all feels very very far away. The Fens have a disturbing beauty. I've nearly driven the car off the road countless times, my eyes drawn into the siren distance that I'm sure you can never master. The people in the parish put homemade marmalade, bags of sugar, sweets and some baked beans in the fireplace and there was a card welcoming us. Several weathered faces have also been round with punnets full of strawberries, tasting of England and childhood. It's easy to believe, especially with the generous sunshine, that this is merely a holiday and that this is a land where fruit and flowers flow. I know the winter is endless. I would imagine it's not called the forbidden zone for nothing.

My only plans are to have no plans. I have this hope that God will fill this space, that this time here may be gentle and that I may truly come to love the people and the long straight roads that narrow in the distance. Back to the boxes, only another forty to go.

I'm off on retreat in two days' time. The list has also arrived containing the names of those being ordained on Sunday. I am the only one who hasn't attended university. They all have initials after their names which could well be some exotic sexually transmitted disease for all I know. The media are rattling on again about disestablishment. Prince Charles apparently wants to represent all faiths; did Christ represent all faiths? Did Allah, Krishna? Did they represent all faiths? Or are they all faiths? The trouble with blending too many flavours, as any cook will tell you, is that ultimately you cannot taste anything.

Did God intend this? Are we all to be the same, say the same things, worship in the same way? The diversity within the Christian camp provides us with some very different views of God. Translated on to a world stage, can Christians really rest assured that vegetarian pagans worshipping the moon are further from God than they are?

Our lives, I feel, are constructed on seconds and it is our faith in those moments of meaning that illuminate who we are. What we carry around with us is no more than a few shapshots taken in time. When those memories of ourselves are shaken or challenged by a different view of perfection our self-image is affected and it is to a great extent the sounding board of others, of the sky, the sea, that determines who we are. We are reaching constantly into our environment and that environment reacts to us. To behave as if we are connected to nothing will reap us nothingness, oblivion. In denying other life we simply succeed in denying our own. The media devalues our self-image, soundbite culture feasts on us all for its pounds of flesh. The media has turned the terror of famine into a freak show. We watch relieved, rather like the zebras who can stand and watch one of their number being eaten. It must be the ultimate feeling of security. Our politicians have become entertainers; war has become the ultimate spectator sport. Life and death have become something we view rather than do and the more we view the less we do.

Religion may have been 'the opium of the people' in Marx's day but it is television and the national press that under the illusion of care and concern have tethered us to their versions of reality and what is important. We are a siren society. The siren sings, we respond. It's taught us to. As long as you believe religion is for wimps and Christ was an insignificant Jewish minstrel then it will not harm you, affect you even. This is an old-fashioned power battle with the media intent on destroying the credibility of anyone or anything that disagrees with its version of events.

Poacher called, he was ordained last Sunday, he chuckled a lot and said that he and the others on the ordination retreat had been told off for talking and that he'd just managed to calm down about it by the time the Bishop put his hands on his head. We talked about who'd be next but they all seemed to be drifting out of sight like balloons let go in the wind.

July 1994

I'm on the ordination retreat. We've spent a lot of time jumping in and out of cassocks. The Bishop seems well on the bus, he speaks slowly and softly. He was the one at the front of the class at school. We've done the usual things, sit around in a huddle and introduce ourselves. We're all in silence now, there's no talking until ten forty-five tomorrow. There are twelve of us being ordained: seven people are to be ordained priest and five deacons. We filed along the road into the cathedral for Evensong, a full choral Evensong. It was mind-blowing, all this for God, all this for each other. The cathedral was busy, tall. There was a constant criss-crossing of people through the vast space after the service. There was a guest choir from Poland and together with the regular choir we were treated to the second movement of Handel's 'Messiah', maximum volume. Except for the Bishop's squeaky sandals and the occasional plane we're wrapped in silence now. Listening to an aural film and the astonishing rapture of the birds singing out the end of the day.

I've become acutely aware on this retreat how much has been done for me, and of everything that I have in my usual callousness taken for granted. The teaching freely given, the patient enduring, the buildings of quiet, the still flowers, the prayers over the years. Cathedrals inspire a sense of gratitude and although the shock of the dynamics and the blazing blue of the stained-glass windows is dulled by the assault on our senses from every angle, the idea remains the same, the idea that God is like this, ornate, grand, awesome;

with the echoes of the choirs dripping from the roof, it's difficult not to draw any conclusions regarding heaven. There were twenty-two observers at Evensong watching the medieval ritual unfold; they were no more than tourists sucked into a flash of flowing cassocks laced with an untouchable God. They could not know that beauty has blood all over it and, as the Bishop reminded us today, conflict lies at the very heart of our human faith. We cannot pretend otherwise. To avoid the conflict, to paper over the problems, simply gives the rot more wood.

The trouble is we have taken love for granted; we have assumed that love is our right as human beings along with clean air and water. We have assumed it's instinctive. We have fallen for the French view of romance; we have entrusted this most precious of commodities for safe-keeping into the arms of adolescence and onto the lips of actors and wide-eyed animated chipmunks. We have assumed that love can be learned along with spelling, that honesty can be instilled with respect and discipline. We have forgotten the lessons of love and more fundamentally that there is only one teacher and that teacher is Christ. Without Christ's definition of love we are destined for hell. To live in hell. When that love is denied the results are plain to see.

None of this was entered into at college. Maybe they assumed we knew it. The teaching here has been extraordinarily good. I'm ordained the day after tomorrow. I really do simply want to be alone. These times on retreat are priceless. My life is punctuated by them, punctured by them. We are in silence again. It has been one of those still English evenings, the cathedral tower watered by the dusk. There is even a scent of roses in the air.

Tomorrow we have some legal business to do in the Chapel; we're given our licences. The Bishop, who has been quite brilliant, left us this evening with the instructions to enjoy our calling and that if we achieve the legacy of the mystery of humility in our ministry not so much can go wrong. We had a rehearsal this evening after another sensual helping of Evensong. The Dean marched us up and down, organized us into rows and told us how hot it was. The Cathedral is a pregnant place, distinguished by its poverty and staggering ceilings. There is always something that you haven't noticed.

I really lost control at the end of hymn 574; it has been a good friend to me and I would sing it loudly in the mornings when I was walking into college. To have it in this setting broke me completely. I wept uncontrollably for a while. The priest next to me put his hand on my shoulder.

This has been a marvellous journey. The God I now know is quite different from the one I started with. I'm not quite sure who has changed. I have a feeling neither of us has, it was perhaps never necessary, just an illusion like so many that dance in front of us. The God I have met has forced me to confront my own pain. The distance I create between that God and myself. Within that confrontation I have discovered parts of myself that I didn't know existed and in doing so I have learned to value them less. I'm not convinced God is an individual being like ourselves. We see him in those terms perhaps because we have no other reference for him other than our immediate understanding of life. The I God uses is corporate, plural perhaps, in form, in being, and it is here in this fourth dimension that we see the staggering beauty of the Trinity.

I crept out of my room and scrambled up onto the wobbling roof of a bicycle rack; on the other side of the fence was a swimming pool. It was dark; I took all my clothes off and dived in. I've just come back. I'm going to try and go to sleep now.

2 July 1994

I was close to tears for much of the time. The actual ordination, the part where the Bishop put his hands on my head, was immensely humbling. I remember looking at my wife, she looked so beautiful among the smiles of my friends. As an event it is padded with pomp and colour; it's designed to be impressive, orchestrated to overpower the observer with the Christian version of the reality of life. When it was all over we went out to the front of the cathedral and had our pictures taken. The bit I really remember was driving back through the Fens, the road was absolutely straight, the ghosts of cars were drifting through the heat flooding the horizon and the still green fields on either side disappeared into the sky. The music was very loud and the windows were all open. We were going to another world.